AF441812

The Professional Secretary

The Professional Secretary

Skills and Techniques for Recognition and Success

Diane Daniels
Ann Barron

amacom

American Management Associations

Library of Congress Cataloging in Publication Data

Daniels, Diane.
  The professional secretary.

  Bibliography: p.
  1. Secretaries—Handbooks, manuals, etc.   I. Barron,
Ann.   II. Title.
HF5547.5.D36   651.3'741'0202   82–71312
ISBN 0-814-5599-9   AACR 2

First Printing

Preface

"Oh, I'm just a secretary," she'll say when the talk gets around to "And what do you do?" It's said in much the same way a woman will announce that she's "just a housewife"—deprecating, apologetic, sometimes defensive that in this day and age she has not become a world beater, a lawyer, a brain surgeon, a fire fighter, or a manager. She's "just a secretary."

With all the ferment caused by the women's movement, with more women than ever in or entering the workforce, pressures are on to get the so-called big jobs: "Don't be a secretary; have a secretary" counseled the parents of a friend.

But the fact remains that there's never that much room at the top for men or women—even now, especially for women. Here are those same old figures again: Most women in the workforce have jobs with low pay and little status. A recent Bureau of Labor Statistics report stated that "the largest single occupational group among women today is still the clerical one—stenographers, typists, secretaries—a category that first gained prominence among women in the 1920s and 1930s and continued to grow after World War II."

In May 1979, according to the report, 80 percent of *all* (emphasis ours) clerical workers were women and 99.1 percent of secretaries were women. In 1950, female clerical workers numbered 62 percent, and in 1962, 98.5 percent of secretaries were women.

"Over time, also," writes Louise Kapp Howe in *Pink Collar Workers,* "as technology progressed, we have seen some occupations formerly on male turf (clerical work is the largest example) broken up into smaller parts and then gallantly handed over (along with the new machines and half the wages previously paid to men) to women, and where equal-pay-for-equal-work laws are of little or no meaning, since if women are competing with anyone for these jobs they are competing with other women."

In recent months increased publicity over unionization of all clerical workers raises again the need for altered attitudes about "women's work."

As syndicated columnist Ellen Goodman wrote recently: "In this time of change, when the status and stroking of society have gone to the innovators, how many others have felt left behind: 'just' a teacher, nurse, secretary, homemaker? . . . The fact is that a rise in status for women is associated, for better or for worse, with entry into the male world. The caretakers, those who are helpers, nurturers, teachers, mothers (and, we might add, secretaries) are still systematically devalued."

We are concerned specifically in this book with the 3 million secretaries in this country who have few books written for them other than office procedure manuals or an occasional chapter in "management" books telling them how to "escape."

Employers across the country report they are having a hard time finding secretaries. The U.S. Bureau of Labor Statistics predicts that openings in the secretarial fields will continue to increase rapidly. Secretaries are in short supply. Management seems willing to go to great lengths to get and keep top management people, but often balks at paying a top secretary what she's worth.

Sentiment runs strong against unions for secretaries among the women attending the seminars. But it may not stay that way without certain changes in the field.

Secretaries repeatedly define their work as "making my boss more efficient—seeing that the office runs smoothly so he can do a good job." This book is for those secretaries who need someone to make them look good; to make their days run smoothly; to increase their efficiency. *The Professional Secretary* is frankly pro-secretary: It's for those who wish to remain and advance in the field and acquire a professional status.

At the top rung in the secretarial field are the executive secretaries and the administrative assistants. While we hope that *The Profes-*

sional Secretary will offer something of interest to all secretaries, we are most concerned with those looking for a career in the field. Our experience over the last four years convinces us that although many do, indeed, wish to "escape," many more would remain in the field if they commanded professional respect and were offered increased responsibilities and tangible recognition—which includes, but is not limited to, higher salaries.

We hope in *The Professional Secretary* to show secretaries methods of managing their jobs and themselves that will point the way to success in the field they have chosen.

If we always use "she" as the secretarial pronoun, it's because statistics are on our side, as we reported earlier. If we more times than we like use "he" for the boss/executive, it's to avoid confusion. Constant repetition of he/she and him/her becomes cumbersome. We do write it that way whenever we can.

Just a secretary? Like all people, secretaries "need growth, initiative, respect, personal satisfaction, and money. With these no one is a 'just,' " Goodman states. We agree.

Diane Daniels
Ann Barron

Contents

x   CONTENTS

Part I

Conceptions and Misconceptions

1

Portrait of a Secretary

SECRETARIAL LEVELS

The title of secretary has been given to people who function up and down the career ladder from typist to administrative assistant, but in most places, receptionists and clerk-typists are at a lower level. They deal with visitors and phone callers, make appointments, and file. Stenographers have an added skill, but may be part of a stenographic pool, limited to taking dictation and transcribing letters for a number of people.

A secretary is more of a generalist. She usually works for one person; seldom more than two people. Generally she needs stenographic and typing skills, but she must be able to do much more. Duties may include opening and routing the mail, ordering supplies, filing, answering the phone, setting up appointments and meetings, typing correspondence and other written communications, setting up travel itineraries, handling payroll for specific sections, and handling petty cash funds.

Most secretaries are capable of handling many and varied responsibilities. Over and above attending to the routine duties mentioned above, in large organizations they often lend administrative support by putting material together for reports and extensive memos, keeping confidential files, keeping people informed on matters of policy, doing research for presentations, and composing and dictating some correspondence.

Here's where the line between secretary and administrative secretary blurs in some organizations. With the advent of word processing, secretaries are beginning to run on two separate tracks, functioning as administrative secretaries or as word processing or correspondence secretaries/document producers. The administrative secretary attends to scheduling, attends meetings, takes dictation, does research, and attends to other administrative details, whereas the correspondence secretary handles all the typing needs of the departments connected with the word processing center.

Briefly, in administrative secretarial centers that use word processing, several secretaries work with a group of executives in handling business mail, phone communications, records, and files. Such centers stress the importance of a secretary who exercises initiative and creativity in all areas of communication; require proficiency in editing, proofreading, and research techniques; and emphasize the ability to plan, organize, and schedule work priorities.

Such a secretary is often called an executive secretary or administrative assistant. She needs to have a thorough knowledge of the executive's job responsibilities and to be willing and able to make certain executive decisions. Of course, she can't function properly in this way unless she works for an executive who is confident enough to delegate meaningful duties to her.

Some secretaries elect to work in fields in which they need a working knowledge of a specialized terminology and procedures. This is true of the legal secretary, who, in some cases, holds a notary's commission. If she works in a small office, she is often an apprentice or paralegal aide. Even if she isn't, she may manage much of the routine of the legal practice.

The medical secretary probably has a wider variety of options than those with other specialties. She needs proficiency in medical terminology, medical shorthand, and medical office procedures. As with the legal secretary, her duties will vary with the size of the organization for which she works. In preparation for a medical secretarial career, the secretary should know how to maintain financial records, insurance forms, and accounting records and be sympathetic and discreet in guarding confidential matters.

The technical secretary may prepare technical correspondence and reports for an engineering firm, or she may type tabulations or chemical or mathematical formulas, using special characters. A knowledge of basic accounting and a familiarity with scientific terminology are necessary. Some background in the physical sciences is also helpful.

Growing in demand and numbers is the certified professional secretary or CPS.* The CPS has passed a comprehensive exam and may be considered a certified professional. In Chapter 12, we'll look at the CPS option as one way to professionalize the secretarial role. We'll also include information about the test, where to take it, and what to study in preparation (see Appendix).

But to get a better idea of what it means to be a secretary, let's hear from some secretaries on how they view their jobs.

SECRETARIAL PROFILES

What is a secretary really like? Is she the way movies and television have portrayed her over the years—a model of cool efficiency called Miss or Mrs., usually an older woman guarding the Official Presence with all the ferocity of a mother cat? Or is she a bubble-haired, bubble-headed, bubble gum-chewing, invariably blonde, buxom creature made for chasing around desks?

We've yet to run into either the Dragon Lady or the "girl." A typical secretary—a Hollywood TV sitcom secretary—does not exist any more than a Hollywood TV sitcom executive, lawyer, doctor, or teacher does, so we won't attempt a composite portrait. We will, instead, give you a look at some secretaries we have met across the country and show you what they're like in all their human complexity.

The secretary is likely to be a high school graduate with some business courses to her credit. Some, of course, are college graduates, and many have gone to college for a few years. Some have gone into secretarial work after pursuing studies in liberal arts and being unable to find work in their field. Some secretaries have done advanced study or are now going back to school.

Carol Oliver, employed by a large West Coast company, is one secretary who didn't just drift into the field. Now 27, Carol was in a

* CPS is a registered service mark of the Professional Secretaries International Association.

work study program in high school when she worked as a secretary and decided she "loved it. I knew that's what I wanted to do right away." Carol thinks she's a "good organizer" and many secretaries claim the same skill.

A strong belief in the work ethic motivates most of them.

"I don't believe in the dole," Caroline Parker, from the international division of an Indiana-based company, said. "I was raised to do what was expected of me and knew I would have to earn my own living." Caroline is not alone in this attitude; we heard it expressed frequently.

Margaret Hennig and Anne Jardim, authors of *The Managerial Woman,* report that the 25 women profiled in their book all had fathers with essentially "male," or not sexually based, high expectations for them.

"All," write Hennig and Jardim, "had had extremely close relationships with their fathers and had been involved in an unusually wide range of traditionally masculine activities in the company of their fathers, beginning when they were very young."

We don't want to make too much of this, but most of the secretaries we interviewed did not have similar experiences. But, of course, many say that going to college or having a career (as opposed to simply earning a living) wasn't the norm for either the males or females in the family.

Rule-oriented, unadventurous, essentially secure is how many describe their backgrounds. But today the same women claim unhappiness with what they believe is their inability to express themselves on the job. Unrebellious by background or training, they sometimes feel they are ineffective communicators. (This may be changing among some younger, more politically oriented women.)

Consider Sara Emerson and Rebecca Saunders. Close to each other in age, both Sara and Rebecca could be classified as ambitious, bright, achieving. Sara, who is politically oriented, speaks hip, up-to-the-minute language, dresses casually, and seems unafraid to express herself, publicly or privately. Rebecca, a recently promoted administrative assistant, wears neat but chic office-style clothes, knows her work, likes her boss, but feels caught between her ambitions and her need for a personal life.

"I have a good life with my husband," she said. "We have many things we enjoy doing on weekends. I don't mind working on Saturday mornings but he (her boss) doesn't want to get started until the afternoons."

Sara has found her own spot in a large corporation to, in her word, "impact." Involved in group dynamics and functioning as a leader, she is at her happiest in problem-solving situations. Competitive and occasionally aggressive—"I'm not afraid to be aggressive rather than assertive when the need arises"—Sara believes in "discipline"; years spent in a quasi-military girls organization and in the Armed Forces give her a no-nonsense attitude overlaid with a lot of current psychological jargon.

Rebecca is moving up. Her need is to come to grips with how far she wants to go. In many ways, she feels a desire to stay where she's been. Vulnerable now and "responsible," Rebecca worries about being held accountable. Sara seems to have no such worries but is in a different work situation.

How can they both be helped? What are their differing needs? Rebecca has many managerial skills: She can plan, organize, delegate, and supervise, but she needs more self-confidence, more daring, and more risk-taking ability, if—and only Rebecca can decide—she wants an expanded career.

Sara's ambitions seem more difficult to define. The area of human relations, race relations, and interpersonal groups in which she works is new to many companies. Yet it is hard to see her as a team player.

How can they both be considered "secretaries"? The word itself (originally, it meant someone entrusted with secrets) seems to be undergoing significant changes in definition. Is an administrative assistant just a glorified secretary with a title but not much more money? Is Sara, carving her own niche in her own section of a big corporation, the same as the woman who takes dictation, types letters, files information, answers phones, and maybe even carries a cup of coffee to her boss? How are the technological advances such as word processing and others yet to come changing the field? And what about the push by the Professional Secretaries International Association for certified professional secretaries, a status achieved by passing a comprehensive test?

Sherry is employed by a Bible Belt religious publisher who is given to temper tantrums, "hollering" imperiously for Sherry from his office to hers any time he wants. "Sherry, get in here. . . . I need you!" she quotes him.

Jean, a veteran of 25 years with the same organization, has hit top pay for her job. She tells of her difficulty in getting reports back on time from middle managers in the company, a task she's been assigned by her boss, the vice-president of communications of a large Chicago-based firm.

"I know it's because they're also pressured and overworked, but it's my job to get the reports back on time and I don't want to fail. I can't help wondering if I'm forceful enough with them or if they believe it's easy to put me off because I'm just a secretary without any real power."

Others report the same difficulty. "Nobody listens to you if you're just a secretary," Kristin Falkner, who works for a large advertising agency, claims. It points up the trouble many secretaries have in speaking up authoritatively. Is there a solution to this problem?

April Harte, who at first glance seems to have no difficulty "speaking up," wonders why she cannot get attention for her ideas at the board meetings she sometimes attends.

"Even when I wear my 'strong suit' nobody listens to me," she complained.

April's "strong suit": a severe navy blue suit of awkward length, buttoned-to-the-neck white blouse with self-tie, sensible shoes. Having learned the "dress for success" look, she applied it literally and somehow aggressively. Almost a parody of the business woman, April achieved an effect that was slightly intimidating. But later, in a role-playing situation, April, who moved, dressed, and talked authoritatively, suddenly crumpled and pleaded "please, please" in seeking the cooperation of a reluctant co-worker. Again, what's the problem?

"I'm not a religious person," Janet Jackson, who works for a neighborhood organization founded in the early civil rights days, said, "but I don't like to lie. My boss asks me to lie to his creditors all the time, telling them that 'the check is in the mail.' It's getting so that they all know me by name and I know them. These are not even business expenses he's lying about . . . they're for the suits he's wearing and the meals he's eaten." How can Janet handle this? Or listen to Bonnie Martin's experience as a legal secretary. (Bonnie is now a law student.)

> There was all the lying on the phone to clients they (the lawyers) didn't want to talk to. "Tell them I'm with a client," they'd say, and the person I was on the phone with would yell "Don't give me that crap, I just called two minutes ago." Or one, who had been trying all day to reach her lawyer, finally said, "I'm going to call every ten minutes until he speaks to me."
>
> But the worst came when I found that my boss was cheating the government. He also acted as a federal magistrate and was supposed to put in for my pay the hours I worked every month. Well, I discovered the records after I'd been there for a while and he was charging the government for the maximum amount of time allowable for my salary when I actually didn't work anywhere near those hours. I didn't know what to do about it. I asked the other secretary if she knew and she said she did. But she was in her sixties and afraid of losing her job if she confronted him with it. It seems funny to me now that I could also have been so afraid.

Bonnie debated her course of action and finally wrote her boss a letter.

"It's because he was so persuasive a lawyer that I did it that way. I didn't want to take the chance that he could convince me he was right."

Before she could send the letter to him, he heard her discussing it with the other secretary and demanded to see it.

> He told me it (falsifying the records) was like taking certain deductions on your income tax . . . that it was in a gray area legally . . . that the magistrate's salary was so low a certain amount of padding was expected. One of the things I worried about before I decided what to do was getting him into real trouble where he wouldn't be able to support his family. I didn't want to do that but . . . it was a real ethical dilemma for me.

Anyway, he agreed to stop falsifying the records, and
he did. But after I left for law school I heard that he
went right back to it. I figure he netted about $400 extra
a month over a good many years.

How should Bonnie and Janet handle lying? What does a secretary or any employee owe a boss? What about questions of loyalty? How can you avoid being intimidated?

Others report disorganized bosses.

"I never wanted to be a secretary," Shanna Wilson said. Shanna, 36, divorced and mother of a six-year-old daughter, works for the director of psychiatric services of a growing suburban hospital. She has had several years of college and has worked "at all kinds of jobs—mainly in offices but not secretarial."

Although she likes her current boss, Shanna maintains that he is not an administrator. "If the hospital would approve the position, I should be appointed his administrative assistant. This would allow him to function at what he does best—psychiatry." As it is, Shanna is a kind of acting administrative assistant, unofficially and with no real authority. "I see what needs to be done and I do it," she said. "It's an accepted fact around the hospital that I run that department. I'm a superorganized person and he's not."

Because her status as administrative assistant has no official sanction, Shanna is often uncertain of how far she can go. A recent episode involving a code call (a call to alert specified people in the hospital that an emergency situation exists) is a case in point. Shanna took it upon herself, in the absence of any authorized person and under what she deemed to be an emergency situation, to issue a code call. Her boss angrily cited her lack of authority. Shanna reminded him that their department had no clear-cut policy on code calls.

The upshot came when, after much procrastination by the boss, Shanna drafted a policy that will, when approved by the hospital's policy committee, be adopted. Writing policy is surely a management function. Shanna earns slightly more than $10,000 a year (1979) and is an hourly employee. Overtime has been drastically curtailed by the hospital in the current cost-cutting climate, and Shanna barely makes ends meet.

A black secretary rising rapidly in a large firm has a different sort of problem: she believes she must be better than anyone else. Employed by the same firm as Sara, a firm that has gone in for human relations, black/white relations, and black literature courses for its employees because affirmative action policies have altered its workforce, Iris Walton is still fearful.

Caroline is in line for promotion out of secretarial work and into a first-line supervisory job:

> I'm not sure it's what I want to do. I've seen what happens to women in those jobs here. They feel they must work twice as hard as the men in order to prove themselves. They take briefcases full of work home every night and every weekend to keep up the impression of hard work. If they don't, they are not taken seriously. The men don't do it. I don't know if that's the kind of life I want, but I've gotten as far as I can go in the secretarial field unless they create a new position for me. It's being discussed. Actually my work as a secretary is much more interesting and varied than the work the first-line supervisors do."

Caroline has some of the same decisions to make as Rebecca. Are the risks of an upwardly mobile career worth taking? "What will I gain? What will I lose? What do I want, anyway?"

Ilona Bergman works for a music distributor. She tells of a job so fragmented that management of her time seems impossible. "I'm a fire fighter," she says.

Ilona claims her days are without shape, impossible to organize, a dance from crisis to crisis. She cannot set goals for herself or bring any structure into her job because of the nature of her duties. Ilona told us she wanted a book that offered some solutions, some help with her day, some way to professionalize the secretarial career. But she herself wryly mentioned the boss who sees secretaries as status symbols. He likes to see her sitting there taking his dictation and often won't use a dictaphone or tape. "He's afraid he'll lose his little tweetie taking notes," she said.

Small problems abound:

"I'm not the important one in that office," Marian Windsor said, speaking of a situation in which she does not have access to the mail or papers because her boss locks them up in his office.

"My boss won't let me delegate any of my work," said another. "When I'm gone it piles up and piles up. It's more than I can get done but he won't hire anybody to help."

An older secretary tells of being trained in the "phone game," the old standard keep-the-other-boss-hanging-waiting-for-your-boss routine. "I'm surprised to see some of the younger people still doing it," she said.

More serious is the problem of intimidation.

"The fear comes in confronting the authority figures in the office," according to Bonnie. "It's just something that comes over you when you're in that situation. You know they have the authority and you don't. There are many little ways you're reminded of that over and over as a secretary. For example, one lawyer had a secretary 15 years older than he and he called her by her first name but insisted that he be called mister."

All the situations these secretaries describe present real problems, many of which the secretary can solve alone or in cooperation with her boss. Skills of time management, communication techniques, assertive responses, job descriptions, written standards of performance, and specific goals and objectives, both business and personal, are all tangible and obtainable. But—is the game worth the candle?

In article after article we read about the discontent permeating the field, about the woman behind the typewriter, in front of the executive's door, face as carefully composed as her letters, who is no longer happy to stay in her "mindless" and "ego-destroying" role. That's how the power broker Michael Korda characterizes the secretarial position. Others label the secretary the "Achilles heel of the women's movement."

What seems to be missing in these descriptions is a look at the secretary as she exists, in a small southern town, a large midwestern corporation, a lawyer's office, an advertising agency, or the executive suite.

"I think the biggest problem secretaries have is with their self-image," said Ronald Medows, vice-president of communications for a large Chicago-based firm. "Women's lib is responsible for much of that. Somehow it gave secretaries and housewives the idea that their work is somewhat degrading. I think that's nonsense. I know some managers who need greater sensitivity, but the biggest problem is how they (secretaries) see themselves."

It is not our intention here to criticize the women's movement, but only to say that statements about Achilles heels seem counterproductive to us. In our experience, about half of all the secretaries attending seminars and roughly the same percentage of those we have interviewed at greater length like being secretaries—do feel the game is worth the candle. That is not to say there's no discontent in the ranks, or that all are strong, unsung heroines with no Achilles heels, but most see their jobs as important to their bosses and their organizations.

Often, however, this is not accompanied by a concomitant ability to assert this value to others. Although their biggest problem may be "how they see themselves," as Medows claims, that feeling often arises because of how they believe others view them. In effect, they get there first with the "I'm just a secretary" routine. Of course, we recognize the self-image problem, but one source is society's attitudes.

According to Roy Rowan, writing in *Fortune* magazine, March 1979, the executive secretary's power "depends on the degree of confidence the boss places in her ability and judgment, and this cannot always be measured by the size of her paycheck. A lot too depends on her own ambition and ego."

To present either picture—the secretary as victim, performing "mindless, ego-destroying work" while fomenting revolution behind the back of her boss or as Miss Cool Efficiency, self-effacing, fiercely protective, the power behind, and so on—is once again to ignore the human complexities of the people involved and their situations.

Where do you place Ilona in all this, for example? An attractive blonde who graduated from college as a history major, she says, "I like being a secretary. I don't mind being told what to do." Or Rebecca, the new administrative assistant, crisp as a dollar bill, who worries about the Peter Principle. "When I was a secretary, if I failed at something, I said to myself, 'Oh well, I'm just a secretary, what can they expect?' But now. . . ." Underneath the apprehension she seems excited, however.

There's Caroline, who is also excited about her work: "I get personal satisfaction out of making my boss more effective." But, she adds, "I do get recognition for the work I do. I demand it."

And Coralee Andrews, giving off energy like a dynamo, who has ambitions to become a swim coach and claims to have a copy of the ad "Let's Get Rid of 'The Girl.' "* above her desk right outside the president's office. "I got a little flak at first," she said, "But it's better now."

But Bailey Carnes, young and not long out of high school, complains about boredom. "Some days I just sit and doodle. . . . Then they give me busy work. 'Clean up those dirty old files.' I want to get out."

There are those, of course, who do get out, like the veteran ten-year secretary writing in the *Chicago Sun-Times* recently about employers' attitudes, insensitivities, slights, all the small things that wound, and then the ritual recognition flowers during secretaries week. "I quit," she announced.

Many do quit. Even those who like their jobs admit to a "lack of respect from others." In Caroline's words: "We're looked at as 'just a secretary.' I notice my boss didn't steer his daughter into the field."

Let's let those who have stayed in the field talk some more about themselves, their bosses, and their work. Kristin, who is always being told she looks just like a secretary—"What exactly does that mean, I look like a secretary? Is it because I'm young or blonde or what?"—was joined by Leslie Lambert, Connie Warden, and Pam Braddock for a lunchtime job discussion one day.

More respect, more responsibility, more recognition—the old lament repeated again over the spinach salad.

"I want to be proud to say I'm a secretary," said Leslie, who has spent eight years with an ad agency in New York. "We need more respect for the work we do," Pam said, and added that she functions more as an unofficial administrative assistant than as a secretary. (Pam later left the agency for a move to California.)

They all agreed that they would rather not say they were secretaries; it was the "I'm just a secretary" syndrome again, but—

* United Technologies made the ad available free to those writing to Harry J. Gray, United Technologies(S), Box 360, Hartford, CT 06141.

important point—based on *other* people's perceptions. They were aware of the value of the work they do, and they believed their bosses were also—*their* bosses—but not other bosses in the same organization.

Three of the four professed great fondness for the men they worked for. "I really love those two guys," said Connie, a tall woman, with a Lauren Hutton gap between her two front teeth. Connie, who wants to be a comedienne, is a graduate of a local theater group and also does some comedy writing. "I consider that the three of us work together," she said, underlining "together," and "all three of us work for the same company"—a major point for her.

The company. It seems to be what keeps the four of them in their jobs even though they know the money's better at other places in the city. (Since this discussion, the dissatisfaction with salaries, inadequate performance evaluations, and lack of merit increases is becoming greater than the pleasure in working for the company, according to Leslie. Concern about the situation has reached the top, because the organization is losing secretaries.)

"We know women who have left here and gone other places but have come back. It's friendly and informal. They're not sticky about breaks *if* you get your work done. That's what they care about. We help each other out with our workloads. It's fun to come to work. Of course, we get to see the end result of our work and say 'I worked on that commercial.' I don't know if I'd want to work at other, stuffier places," said Kristin, who has been with the agency for two years.

"I like responding to deadlines," Leslie said. And in that business, deadline pressure is common.

But Pam admitted to being bored. "I need more responsibility. My goal right now is to go back to school. I don't know. Maybe I'll get into word processing, which could lead to computer work."

"I work for one man, who really is the nicest person," Pam continued. "When I first started working for him, everything was in a mess. I had to ask him for time to get it organized. Now I am more of an administrative assistant than a secretary."

Organizing, a knack for detail—Leslie reports liking that part of secretarial work, as do many others. Connie asks how she can get recognition for having taken on one of her boss's responsibilities. Kristin complains about not being listened to. Leslie tells of how she is stuck doing personal chores for her boss.

"It's my fault for not saying no at the beginning, but my boss always did expect personal work. I think he believes it's one of the things he's entitled to—that he's so valuable to the company he deserves it."

In general, though, the women agreed that, at least at their agency, secretaries were asked to take care of personal chores for bosses far less frequently than they had been in the past. Kristin said she didn't mind. She felt as if "I'm doing a favor and they would do one for me."

Other things may also be different. The four report that "Older secretaries at the company are often secretive about the work they do. They won't give or accept help from other secretaries. 'It's confidential,' they'll say." "I figure we all work for the same place," was Connie's reaction.

And how does Leslie feel about the place—Leslie, who has thought frequently about a job in the "creative end" of the agency? "I would like to stay here if I could earn enough. I'm at the ceiling now, though. Maybe a title change. . . ."

Half a continent away from the ad agency, another conversation took place, this one at the corporate headquarters of a large, diversified business with offices throughout the country—and thousands of employees. In many ways the human beings seemed an intrusion in the almost reverent atmosphere. Modern typewriters do not clatter; phones ring discreetly; carpeting muffles the sound of heels. All the visible flooring gleams with a high polish: wood, of course. Offices are large and uncluttered; whole other areas are given over to plush couches, coffee tables, lamps, artwork, and, of course, the View.

From that high up, the boats on the lake looked frozen in time, like a French Impressionist painting from the museum across the street—making another work of art among the paintings and sculpture on display.

Three secretaries and one recently promoted writer-designer met for lunch in the building's restaurant to discuss their jobs, their bosses, themselves, and their future. All were (or had been) top secretaries—meaning that they worked for the senior executives in the corporation. One, Georgia Towers, was the board chairman's secretary; Jean Robbins, small, hair cut in straight bangs, worked for the vice-president of communications; Laura Colman worked for an operational vice-president; and Rachael Simmons, the new writer, had been in the legal department.

Georgia, from Birmingham, England, informs the group that "Secretary is a title you earn in England. It's not downgraded there. I was a shorthand-typist first, doing nothing all day but taking dictation and typing it up. I was *not* considered a secretary. Eventually, I was promoted to secretary."

Georgia has been in America ten years and recently earned her degree from Mundelein College by taking weekend courses. "She gave up all her social life to do it," said her co-workers proudly. "She's now going for her M.B.A."

"I left school at 15 in England . . . failed the tests given to all students at 11 years of age." (The tests determine who will go on for advanced education.)

After ten years in the legal department, Georgia has been with the board chairman for six years. "He's a good delegator," she said. "A little vague about what he wants sometimes, but—in a way—that gives you some leeway. But only if you guess right," she added, with a smile.

They were discussing what makes a good boss. Georgia said a good boss "delegates, trusts you, will turn over projects to you and then leave you alone to do them, is not always looking over your shoulder." Rachael said she would give her former boss an A−. The talk turned to other, more negative aspects of the job.

Laura said she was "not stimulated" by the work. "I'm not business oriented; things outside my job are more important to me. But my work is a little more interesting now." Laura, a Spanish major in college, found the demand not there in her field and turned to secretarial work when her husband suffered a stroke. Now, she explained, her job is more company oriented; before, she worked eight years for a man for whom she functioned as more of a social secretary.

"But, basically, I feel dulled by the work," she claimed. Rachael had another point of view:

I think there are many attractive things about being a secretary. It's a pleasant way to support yourself, an opportunity to build personal relationships. It was only difficult for me when I was with a group of old college friends who asked "And what do you do?" When I answered that I was a legal secretary, "How interesting," they said in that polite way.

I spent six or seven years of my life thinking I was going to become a college professor. I was first in my class in college, have an M.A. and part of a Ph.D. in history, and am a Phi Beta Kappa. But you know what happened to the market for Ph.D.s. I became a secretary while I figured out what I wanted to do. It offered security, marketability. I could go home at 5 P.M.—I have a small child to care for—and say to my boss "You can stay; you earn a lot more than I do." I decided to get my ego satisfaction elsewhere. It was a conscious decision and it worked.

Secretaries make the corporation run, and are underpaid and undervalued. They are indispensable, irreplaceable, and denigrated. Their talents are unrecognized. Just see what happens when you're not here for a while.

Laura said she didn't like feeling like a maid. "Can you cut this lock of my hair?" one of her bosses once requested. Everybody laughed.

"Somebody I know once found a raincoat and button in the in-box," Rachael said. "Listen," she added, "I've brought my share of coffee to a boss who really expected it and made personal vacation plans for him when I presume his wife also had a phone-dialing finger. I've done it but I don't like it."

"I don't mind doing personal things as a favor," Jean said, "but not as a job requirement."

"I think you should say how you feel," Georgia stated. "I've done it too, but I've always *said* that I didn't like it. It's not good to keep it in. Too many professionals have highfalutin ideas of themselves, and our skills are not equated with theirs in their minds."

"But I feel there *are* highly skilled people—engineers, for example," Laura added, "and I can see where the pay scale comes from."

Although Rachael and Georgia did not disagree with payment for professional skills, they still asserted that the secretary's skills, experience, and loyalty—her contributions—were insufficiently rewarded. Pam told us:

> I would like to see secretaries treated more like professionals than like people who just do the typing and open the mail. There is a lot more involved in being a secretary (and a good one) than most people think. If a boss could sit at a secretary's desk for one day and see what really goes on, I think he or she would be more appreciative of secretaries.
>
> I always hear how hard it is to find a good secretary. I think the main reason for that is the pay scale. Companies will go to any length and pay just about any salary for a good executive. In my opinion, a good executive is no more important than a good secretary. It seems the first place most organizations will cut back when in a crunch is the secretarial staff. People just don't think of secretaries as important.

Some companies are getting the message at last. Organizations without "glamour," where women can't progress into a career in the field, are making their secretarial jobs more desirable. Their job descriptions include increased responsibilities, the title of administrative assistant, and a boost in salary of as much as 30 percent over three years ago. They are responding to a highly competitive market.

It's what we hear over and over again. Office workers' groups talk of the need for Raises, Rights, and Respect. We prefer the three Rs of Respect, Responsibility, and Recognition; of course, recognition encompasses salary increases. The women to whom we have spoken know that salary usually follows respect and increased responsibility.

We have found a touching need among many secretaries to do a good job in order to "make my boss more efficient, to enable him to do a better job." That's their chief job satisfaction, many claim.

We'll end with some generalizations culled from our experiences with more than 1,000 secretaries from coast to coast. As we've mentioned before, most have backgrounds that stressed rules, regulations, responsibilities—work. "My dad ground the idea of work into me," said one. "He told me things aren't always good." Most claim they were easy to raise according to a system of duties and rewards. All sought the respect of their parents.

Intellectually these secretaries want equality with men, but many speak of a lingering need to be cherished. None speak of deprivation. Many uphold loyalty as a prime virtue. The women in the field are people with pride in their skills, pride in their bosses (well, most of the time); people who do not wish to be treated like pieces of furniture or called girls. They are people who balk at doing personal chores for their bosses as a job requirement but will often be glad to do a favor as one human being to another; people who increasingly see themselves as part of a team, contributing not just "ten typing fingers" but also brainpower and ideas.

It gets down to who makes the world go round and what society is willing to pay to keep it running smoothly. Secretaries, who have reached the highest pay scale they've ever had, claim to make the corporations run.

2

Attitudes

They say she's walking—walking for more money, walking even when the money's better than it's ever been before, walking for jobs that offer respect and responsibility and recognition. They say she's making noises about joining or forming unions. At the very least, she's a member of one of the growing number of women's groups around the country, now part of a network known as the National Association of Working Women, with 13 organizations at this writing.

She's the Secretary, and she's said to be in short supply for any number of reasons, money being the prime, but not the only, one. In the late 1970s and early 1980s, the Bureau of Labor Statistics, which records that sort of thing, estimated that secretarial salaries range from $10,353 to $15,693, an increase from the 1978 span of $9,801 to $14,430. A secretarial grouping defined as Class A, ranking right below the executive secretary, who is not included in Bureau figures, earned an average of $15,000 annually in New York City in 1978, $13,000 in the St. Louis region, $10,500 in New Orleans, $13,000 in the Miami area, $16,000 in Seattle, $14,000 in Chicago, $15,000 in Los Angeles, and $13,000 in Cleveland.

A business columnist in the *Chicago Sun-Times* of August 6, 1980, reported that entry-level positions as both administrative secretaries and correspondence secretaries (those who work in word processing centers, who are document producers) averaged $160 per week in 1979, according to a Word Processing Association survey.

Supervisors earned more than $260 a week and managers more than $300. In some places, managers made as much as $500 a week. Stenographers make about $235, and secretaries about $253, or between $13,156 and $13,500 a year. The same survey reported that in 1979, secretaries averaged a 7.4 percent raise and stenographers a 10 percent raise.

A small, unscientific sampling by an airlines magazine of 13 executive secretaries put their salaries at an average of $20,000. The 13 worked for highly placed chief executive officers and professed great love for their jobs. But Manpower, Inc., when it sought to reward top secretarial achievement, discovered once again the prevalance of the "just a secretary" syndrome even at the peak: 38 percent of the recent winners wanted another career; they believed that to be a secretary is to be downgraded.

Money, of course, is only part of the problem, because even with a higher level of salary, women are leaving. But even outside the secretarial field, they'll earn only 59¢ for every dollar paid to men. Figure 1 shows two job descriptions that are circulating through the newsletters of women's groups. Originally published by Working Women, National Association of Office Workers, they compare a "man's job" and a "woman's job" as posted by a major bank. (Banks are a prime target of the women's groups.)

Consider also that the 20 leading occupations for women all involve direct contact with customers/clients and that top secretaries daily perform diplomatic, communications, and organizational tasks for a fraction of their bosses' salaries, and the exodus can be understood.

Understandable—but expensive. Employers facing frequent turnover of employees are paying the price. Estimates put the figure as high as $16,000 to $18,000 for paying and training the average worker until normal productivity is reached. It only makes economic and human sense to see what can be done. We've stated that our goal is to professionalize the secretarial role, to see that secretaries are recognized for what they are—an integral part of the management team. And, of course, recognition involves not only salary, but also the intangible of respect for a co-professional, a person who allows the executive to function at the peak of his capabilities.

What difference will that make to the executive? Well, no guaran-

POSITION: General Clerk

DUTIES: Maintains accounting cost records for all protective equipment installations, removals and service calls; processes RPP records; controls its charges for protective equipment; processes and balances statistical and expense reports; researches materia and projects budget; types correspondence and various statistical reports, technical manuals, purchase orders, and equipment records; analyzes invoices and determines allocation of charges to be expensed or capitalized; assists accounting clerk in maintaining records and accounting procedures of materials and components of sophisticated alarms and other protective devices; answers telephones, takes messages and service calls.

ABILITIES: Excellent statistical and figure aptitude required to compile information, assemble figures and reports, compute and maintain data derived from various sources. General knowledge of accounting and purchasing payables procedures. Must be well organized and able to work independently. Accurate statistical typing. Ability to demonstrate good judgment. Excellent telephone etiquette. Budget and expense experience helpful.

SALARY: $745–$1090

POSITION: Shipping and Receiving Clerk

DUTIES: Perform shipping and receiving duties in the furniture department; receive incoming shipments; assist in unloading; store and deliver items to appropriate location.

ABILITIES: Able to lift equipment in excess of 100 pounds; legible handwriting; no condition or illness which may affect ability to do the job.

SALARY: $1030–$1100

tees, but perhaps the secretarial shortage will slow down, allowing him to get and keep good people. Also, a good secretary, someone once said, is a powerful ally. She is not only an ally, but also a team member capable of independent judgment and initiative. A good secretary is not someone skilled only in the basics, not someone just waiting to be told what to do, but a person who seeks out additional responsibilities. And yes, such a person may prove to be a threat to a boss with a precarious hold on his own sense of power. However, the traditional model of authority and submission is not working in either office or hospital. Witness recent nursing attitude surveys and the nationwide shortage of both nurses and secretaries.

Attitudes change rapidly—inflationary pressures may see to that—but in our experience, the secretary, though feeling strained, considers herself *part* of management and is therefore more resistant to unionization than other workers. Professional career secretaries, earning good money, afforded recognition, given increased responsibilities, can only be an asset, a benefit to a boss and the organization that employs both.

The management loyalty of secretaries should be no cause for smugness. In Boston some members of the "Nine-to-Five" group have joined the Service Employees International. But, in our experience talking to secretaries at seminars around the country, only one out of a thousand would consider joining a union. Whether or not that proves to be a mistake in the long run or whether the statistic holds up in the future, we can't determine here. Although we are not arguing for or against unionization, we know what the prospect does to management's nerves.

If management believes it desirable to avoid unionization, it could pay attention to what members of the combined Working Women group want: job descriptions, regular salary reviews, cost-of-living raises, increased benefits, access to advancement, a grievance system, and the right to refuse doing personal chores for the boss. Anne Ladky, a director of Chicago's Women Employed, lists several suggestions for management, including some already mentioned:

Make a job-content study to show the actual work being done by people.

Assign salary rates for each classification of job after a written job description.
Map out a career path for secretaries.
Hold training programs to upgrade secretaries' skills and allow tuition reimbursement for educational courses.

Will any of this come about—as it has for many other people—without a union? Perhaps someday clerk-typists or those involved in document production might unionize, but will a professional career secretary? At this point we'd guess not, but listen to one secretary, the only male member of the Atlanta chapter of the National Secretaries Association: "Management just doesn't want to pay a top secretary a good salary but management is willing to pay top wages for management people. When is business going to wake up?"

Can the power of the traditional relationship between boss and secretary always be relied on? Or will the secretary succumb forever to the lure of "feeling close to what's going on"? As one secretary told us: "I can talk to vice-presidents. I couldn't do that if I were on the lower rungs of management." That attitude is part of the problem, activists say. But if it's change you want, it will have to start with you. Don't wait for it to come from on high; initiate it on your own. Risky? Yes, but the benefits in respect, responsibility, and recognition will be worth it.

As will be evident in the discussion of the office of the future, a boss will soon need an assistant more than a clerical worker to help cope with the information overload. Be ready. Everybody will benefit from the new professional career secretary.

PROBLEMS

"Don't make this solely a problem book," Ilona requested. Even as she told us it was "hopeless," she asked for help with her day. At the very least, we will try to offer that help plus some concrete management skills, starting with the technical and professional skills that may be considered too basic and elementary to those of you ready to move on but helpful to those just starting out.

At whatever secretarial level you may be, most of you have mentioned problems with your job, your boss, yourself, or your co-workers—problems that often have solutions within your grasp. Well, all right. Perhaps the solutions are within your grasp with a little help from your employer. But fundamentally, you're in control of your own life and job. If change is desirable but not possible where you are, get the skills and move on. You're in demand.

Before you do that, however, think what you would change about your job if you had the power to do just that. What specific work-related problems concern you? From our survey of secretaries attending seminars, we've put together the concerns voiced by about 1,000 women from Boston, Pittsburgh, Washington, D.C., Chicago, New York City, Houston, Atlanta, St. Louis, and Newport Beach, California. Not surprisingly, salary considerations head the list. However, since salary as such is not dealt with in our seminars, greater weight was given to other concerns.

All aspects of time management, scheduling, and organizing of both secretary and boss head the list. Equally important to many is gaining respect and increased responsibility, followed closely by the need for self-assertion. Important to many secretaries, they felt assertiveness was necessary as a way of overcoming the sense of intimidation frequently reported. "I can't keep my boss's attention." "I'd like to avoid being asked to act like a maid." "How can I deal with being the only female in the office?" "I can't express my wishes." "I'd like to overcome the clerical image." We placed these statements in the "how best to assert yourself" category.

Delegating work; how to communicate, to project confidence, to get co-workers to follow through on requests; and setting goals and priorities concerned many. Dealing with co-workers, handling the volume of mail, coping with phone interruptions, coping with multiple bosses, gaining recognition, job title changes or job descriptions, and seeing "the big picture" topped many lists. Some required a technical vocabulary to function more efficiently and many didn't have enough pertinent job information. Teamwork, taking the initiative, dealing with conflict, dealing with questions of loyalty, meeting pressure deadlines, and handling "crash programs" interested many.

Some spoke of bosses who gave vague instructions and could not be pinned down; of bosses unaware of the interference run for them by their secretaries. Others worried about creating a professional image, about defining, communicating, and knowing their own capabilities, about controlling their emotions. Above all, most talked about wanting to grow.

WHAT THE BOSS WANTS

All employees think a lot about their jobs, their bosses, their organizations, and their place in them. Undoubtedly, less thought has been given to *them*. However, we've gathered a list of attitudes, work habits, and other traits bosses wish some secretaries would change:

- Makes too many personal phone calls; conducts too much personal business.
- Doesn't proofread her work.
- Is not self-initiating; doesn't tell me when her workload is light.
- Interrupts me too often, and frequently on trivial matters.
- Doesn't seem to do her job with pleasure, only because she has to.
- Shows lack of interest; poor attitude; is uncooperative.
- Chews gum noisily and excessively, especially under pressure.
- Talks too much, often about unimportant things.
- Comes in late too frequently.
- Fails to keep me informed about meetings, locations, and calendar events.
- Takes too long a lunch too often.
- Waits to be told; doesn't anticipate what needs to be done.
- Bosses other clericals.
- Leaves staples in single sheet after tearing off the top sheet.
- Needs a spelling course.
- Needs memory development.
- Affected in her office work by her personal problems. ("You don't have to ask her if she had a bad night; you *know*.")

A survey of bosses produced the following positive comments about their secretaries:

- Can handle the boss's job when he is away for a few days.
- Anticipates his needs.

- Can run the office: screen calls, schedule appointments, and so on.
- Does excellent filing; is well organized, can find materials when needed.
- Is accurate and neat.
- Is flexible; adjusts readily under pressure.
- Shares responsibility with her boss for follow-up.
- Asks for clarification of any point or asks other questions when in doubt.
- Proofreads the material she types.
- Is interested in content of boss's job; understands the peculiar characteristics of her boss.
- Is cheerful, capable, willing to do what's asked without question.
- Is open-minded.
- Is diplomatic at all times; handles phone calls and visitors graciously.
- Is enthusiastic, thorough, efficient.
- Has good personality and appearance; is willing to learn.
- Has good morale; is agreeable.
- Is able to operate with empathy and understanding without exact instructions.
- Is totally cooperative and willing to assist.
- Is kind and calm.
- Can complete a job with imagination and talent without constantly asking the boss's approach.

WHAT THE BOSS SHOULDN'T DO

Now it's your turn. Here are some things secretaries don't like about their bosses, according to a Professional Secretaries International Association poll:

- Does not inform me where he is going when leaving the office.
- Makes appointments and fails to tell me.
- Dictates late in the day, expecting letters to go out that evening.
- Fails to communicate all the facts.
- Doesn't introduce me to visitors who come into the office.

- Places a phone call and then can't be found when the call is completed.
- Begins projects without preliminary organization.
- Is not a good listener.
- Lacks patience.
- Considers women second-class citizens. (Unfortunately, some women feel the same way.)
- Procrastinates.
- Is moody.
- Is tardy.
- Is sarcastic.
- Has no sense of humor.
- Manages by crisis.
- Never thanks or praises me.
- Doesn't expect enough of me.
- Doesn't give me enough responsibility.
- Doesn't make proper use of my time.

Part II
Job Skills and Where They Lead

3

Technical Skills

Concerned not only with smoothing her boss's day but also with making her own work more significant, today's committed career secretary seeks advancement in her own field and has an increased sense of her value to the efficient functioning of an organization. She realizes that she's part of the management team. Her on-the-job problems, listed in Part I, have solutions in proven management techniques. In Part II we concentrate on specific skills every secretary interested in moving up to an executive secretary or administrative assistant spot should acquire.

We've organized the information into seven categories, starting with the basics—such technical skills as answering the telephone and handling the account books—to administrative skills, communications, interpersonal skills, motivation, leadership, and techniques of problem solving. Some classification could be considered arbitrary and some overlap is inevitable. Problems and solutions don't always line up in neat, mechanical ways, but we believe that in the skills just named lie the answers to your career problems or at least the place to begin looking. Starting with technical skills and moving through to problem solving, we hope to meet the concerns expressed in Part I.

So let's begin with the basics. And what could be more basic, more ubiquitous, than the telephone?

THE TELEPHONE

In some offices it never stops ringing and you're the one who answers it. You deal with all the faceless people who call and interrupt your work. But wait—interrupt your work? More than likely, answering those calls is part of your work, often an important part, however annoying the phone noises become. Although in-person visitors may seem more difficult to handle, phone callers require as much, if not more, tact. All you have is your voice to convey the message. No smile to lessen the disappointment of not getting through, no eye contact, no body language to read. If the caller is unfamiliar with your organization and is a potential client, the phone is often his first introduction to the company. A bad first impression is hard to combat.

And so, because this is all about the basics, let's get very fundamental indeed: It's important to know your equipment. No longer is it just a telephone with a couple of lines and a hold button. As often as not now, it's a *system,* or rather one of several systems, such as Dimension R, Danray, Rolm CBX, Northern Electric, and Stromberg Carlson. Big efficient time-savers, every one.

Most systems have features such as "automatic call back" if a line is busy; "call pickup" for answering another line; "call forward" for transferring your calls to another desk if you are unavailable; and "camp on-busy" to inform you by a burst of tone if a call is in-house or from the outside and if it's important. Many offices now have abbreviated dialing for frequently called numbers. Think of the time you save. Most, if not all, companies conduct in-house classes on the use of any new phone systems being installed. We're sure that secretaries solve their mysteries long before anybody else.

But now, simple or complex, that thing is ringing again. With your pen and pad in had, for the nth time you prepare to follow the hints for phone use outlined below:

• Answer promptly. You could lose business by delay.

• Answer in a helpful manner. Identify your office, your group, your immediate supervisor, or yourself—or any combination of these, depending on what will be helpful to the person calling. You might say "Mr. Scott's Office," or "Purchasing, Ms. McCarthy speaking." If you're a private secretary, it's preferable to give your boss's name rather than the title of the office. It's not necessary to identify yourself unless the caller wants to talk directly to you. It's not good practice to answer with your extension number. There's not much information in "3676."

• Speak distinctly and pleasantly. Your voice often makes the crucial first impression.

• Explain any waiting periods. If you must leave the phone to get information, tell your caller how long you'll be gone and offer to call back. If he waits, get his attention when you return, then give him the information he wants. Remember that it's lonely on hold, even with music.

• Ask questions tactfully. You may have an understanding with your boss requiring you to get the name of any caller. Don't ask bluntly "Who is this?" "May I *ask* who is calling, please?" is preferable to "May I *say* who is calling, please?" which implies that your boss is there. Your boss may not want to talk to the caller. A courteous phrasing of the question will usually elicit a willing answer.

• Know where your employer is. If he's out of town, make sure you know when he's expected to return or where he can be reached.

• Take messages willingly, noting the name of the caller, the phone number, the time, and whether or not he wants to be called back. Repeat the information to make sure it's correct, unless it's confidential, in which case you could ask the caller to repeat it.

• Transfer calls you can't handle, but only if you can't attend to them. No one likes to repeat what he has to say several times before reaching the person who can help him. When transferring calls, signal the operator s-l-o-w-l-y. Transfer only when you're positive of the correct person or number. This is subject, of course, to the system in your office.

• Wrong numbers can be embarrassing. When in doubt, look up the number before you call.

• Be ready to talk when the person you've called answers. Since most calls go through without delay, it's not only courteous, but also saves time.

• After calling a number, give the person at least a minute to reach his telephone.

• As a matter of courtesy, ask if it's convenient to talk. You wouldn't break into a conference in an office. This same rule of etiquette applies over the phone.

• The instrument is tuned to normal voice tones, so don't shout. A loud voice sounds gruff and unpleasant over the phone.

• Identify yourself immediately to the first person answering your call.

• Listen politely and attentively. You wouldn't interrupt a face-to-face conversation. Apply the same rules of etiquette in phone conversations.

• Plan an effective conversation by getting your thoughts in order before a call. Try completing your business in one call by securing the necessary information or by leaving a message.

• The person originating the call usually ends the conversation, unless your company prefers that the customer hang up first.

• And speaking of hanging up—do so gently!

Your biggest problem with phone callers will be the screening process. But if you develop a formula, it won't be as difficult as it sounds. First and obviously, who is on the other end of the line? Remember that if the person hasn't already identified himself, ask whether you may ask who's calling, please. If your instructions are to determine the nature of every call, inquire politely if you may tell your boss what the call is about. What do you do if you get a rude answer akin to "Mind your own business"? Keeping your cool, tell the impolite one that your boss does not take calls before knowing the nature of the call. With experience, you'll learn not to be over-protective. Emergencies do happen; judgment develops as you go along.

Teamwork with your boss plus ongoing communication between you should acquaint you with your boss's priority list, so that you know who he wants to talk to. The order usually is (1) superiors, (2) clients/customers, (3) internal people, (4) suppliers, (5) trade organizations, and (6) friends or personal business calls. Check especially categories (3) and (6).

When you are making a call, be certain that the executive is there and you're not left holding the phone. Keep a record of calls and ask the operator for the tolls and charges.

A variety of long-distance calls are possible:

Conference calls. These, combined with closed-circuit television, may prove to be the airlines' biggest competitor.

Mobile calls.
Overseas calls.
Ship-to-shore as well as *collect* and *credit-card calls.*

Specialized services from the phone company include:

1. Extended Area Service.*
2. Federal Telecommunications System (F.T.S.), linking government agencies, for federal employees only.
3. Foreign Exchange Service (FX), connects customer's telephone to a central office.
4. Bellboy, which buzzes the person.
5. Private Automatic Branch Exchange (PABX), used by hotels and similar industries.
6. Tieline, a service that links offices.
7. Touch Tone, usually linked to a computer that gives bank balances, billing, and credit authorization, and makes reservations.
8. Wide Area Telephone Service (WATS) lines.

This is a standard code for indicating letters:

A	Alfa	N	November
B	Bravo	O	Oscar
C	Charlie	P	Papa
D	Delta	Q	Quebec
E	Echo	R	Romeo
F	Foxtrot	S	Sierra
G	Golf	T	Tango
H	Hotel	U	Uniform
I	India	V	Vicar
J	Juliet	W	Whiskey
K	Kilo	X	X-ray
L	Lima	Y	Yankee
M	Mike	Z	Zulu

* "Extended area service" bills as local calls rather than long-distance calls those made by a company in a city to offices in nearby suburbs.

APPOINTMENTS

One of the greatest responsibilities a secretary has is keeping track of her boss's appointments, deadlines, and items needing follow-up. Some suggestions:

- After you set up appointments for your boss, reconfirm.
- Write down the purpose of the appointment and get a phone number for calling back, subject to your boss's approval. Type a reminder for the person with whom you've made the appointment, stating the date and place. Alternate times may be suggested to the person who wants to see your boss.
- If at all possible, keep Mondays and Fridays light.
- Teamwork with your boss will make this an obvious suggestion, but remember to check with him every morning to avoid setting up duplicate appointments.
- Remind your boss at night and early the next morning of the day's appointments. Use a list or index cards. Put the appointments on both your calendars. Keep a log for expenses and tax purposes.

In spite of the most meticulous planning, checking, and rechecking, two people suddenly appear at the same time for an appointment because of a communications breakdown. What to do? Well, if *you* made the appointment and confirmed it with your boss and *he* also made one without checking with you or his calendar, you may inform him that *your* appointment is waiting. If he says he can't see your person, swallow your embarrassment and either see if someone else can help or reschedule the appointment. A portable schedule for the executive's wallet should prevent this sort of mixup—*if* it's consulted.

A monthly appointment calendar prepared at the beginning of each month and updated as appointments are made or canceled can be helpful. Figure 2 is a simple example. For deadlines, it's wise to put a reminder note on your boss's calendar at least a week before the deadline and another entry on the day the item is due. This helps to avoid last-minute panic and embarrassment.

Above all, anticipate. Thinking ahead marks you as a profes-

Figure 2.   Sample monthly appointment calendar.

Monday	Monday 6	Monday 13	Monday 20	Monday 27
Tuesday	Tuesday 7	Tuesday 14	Tuesday 21	Tuesday 28
Wednesday 1	Wednesday 8	Wednesday 15	Wednesday 22	Wednesday 29
Thursday 2	Thursday 9	Thursday 16	Thursday 23	Thursday 30
Friday 3	Friday 10	Friday 17	Friday 24	Friday 31
Saturday 4	Saturday 11	Saturday 18	Saturday 25	Saturday

sional. Before a scheduled appointment, have all the papers, charts, and graphs your boss will need ready for him.

VISITORS

Office visitors may or may not already be customers/clients. Perhaps they are potential customers. But customers or not, all human beings should be treated with courtesy. As we've mentioned before, a secretary screens visitors and phone calls firmly and efficiently, but without giving offense. The first law is to make sure people who need to get in do get in (or through) and those who don't, don't. Some guesswork is involved, but with experience it can be educated guesswork. Keep these four points in mind:

1. Get the visitor's name, his company, and the purpose of his visit.

2. If he must wait, make him comfortable. Offer reading mate-

rial and coffee if it's available. (If you're sensitive about serving coffee, consider that, in this case, the visitor is essentially a guest.)

3. Decide whom your boss would welcome, whom he does *not* wish to see, who could be seen by someone else, and whom you could take care of yourself.

4. If it's someone your employer does not want to see, be tactful in your explanations.

Tact comes more easily when you have given some thought to what you're going to do in a given situation. Say you're faced with a visitor who won't tell you why he wants to see your boss. Explain that your employer told you he didn't wish to be disturbed today, but if the caller would only say *why* he wanted to see him, an interruption might be possible. Maybe the visitor could be given a little time right now or could be given an appointment for a future date.

If you still can't determine the reason for the visit, ask if you could take a note in to your boss with his name, company, and so on, stating briefly the nature of the visit and requesting an appointment. Be firm but tactful. If nothing works and the visitor persists to the point of rudeness, just repeat that "Mr. Jones sees people by appointment only. I'd be happy to make an appointment for you." You might ask, "Would you be interested in seeing someone else?" or "Can I help you?" Beyond that, there's nothing to do but repeat yourself, without showing any signs of annoyance. In assertiveness training, that's a technique known as "repeating" (for obvious reasons). This technique is also handy to keep in mind when dealing with the press, for instance, when it's after information about the company that's not yet common knowledge. Say "I'm not at liberty to divulge that information," and keep repeating it.

Your boss may be with a client/customer when a competitor walks in unannounced. If you know your boss would not be thrilled to have them meet, politely usher the competitor into a conference room, give him some reading material, and drop a note on the boss's desk.

Your boss may put you on the spot by being late for a scheduled appointment and leaving the fallout up to you. Extend your boss's apologies and ask the visitor if he's able to wait, but don't offer lengthy explanations. Avoid giving the caller the idea that he's not as important as the business that's delaying your boss. Be firm, tactful, polite, and helpful—all of which makes you sound like a

Girl Scout. But better that than an office mother, overprotective and possessive.

In summary: Be as sure as you can be that your boss does not want to see the person you're keeping out. It's a judgment call that can anger. Maybe your boss doesn't want to risk that, so don't overprotect. Try not to give people the impression that you feel your boss is in charge of the world, pressured beyond human understanding or endurance; that nobody else is as busy; that nobody else's time is as valuable; and that they'll get in to see him by crawling over your dead body.

But let us suppose that all the problems are resolved. The visitor is about to get time with your boss. Inform him that "Mr. Jones will see you now" if the visitor is known to your boss. If not, make the introductions yourself, and include the name of the visitor's company as a reminder. You might make up an index card file for your own use with names and pertinent facts about each visitor. It could prove helpful. In addition to your file, keep one for your boss, recording any news stories about his visitors, their preferences, where and when they last lunched, and so forth. As with phone callers, you and your boss should establish a priority list of visitors.

Last, as with the telephone, keep in mind that greeting visitors is part of good public relations. Often you'll be the first person an outsider sees, so the initial impression is important. Your voice, appearance, knowledge of the business, punctuality, and ability to put people at their ease and make them feel important are all crucial. You also have to know how to say "no" politely, assert yourself when necessary with problem visitors, be firm, interrupt wisely, and anticipate. You no doubt do all these things every day without thinking about it. Most good secretaries do.

MAIL

Although the office of the future is supposed to be relatively paperless, the future is not here yet, and the rising tide of magazines, catalogs, and other mail threatens to engulf us. Here's a procedure secretaries can follow to make their mail-handling chores easier and more efficient.

Incoming Mail

1. *Sort all the mail.*
   a. Correspondence
   b. Bills and statements (if they can be distinguished from correspondence at a glance)
   c. Advertisements and circulars
   d. Newspapers and periodicals
2. *Open the correspondence.*
   Stack all the envelopes with flaps up and away from you. Open them all before putting down the letter opener. Remove the contents of each letter. Check that nothing is left in the envelopes.
3. *Attach the enclosures to the letters.*
   If the address of the sender is on the envelope but not on the letter, attach the envelope to the letter. Put all other envelopes aside until all the mail is processed.
4. *Sort the letters into three stacks.*
   a. Those needing your supervisor's attention
   b. Those needing the attention of someone other than your boss
   c. Those requiring your attention
5. *Attend to any correspondence requiring someone else's attention.*
   If necessary, attach the pertinent file or previous correspondence. If you have already attended to part of the letter, mark the paragraph that has had attention. Write the date and "done" or "noted" in the margin and initial. *Note:* Keep a daily record of mail you send to other offices for action. Invaluable as an aid in checking on the receipt and disposition of these letters if follow-up action is needed, your daily record should include the date the material was sent from your office, to whom sent, subject matter, action to be taken, and follow-up date. Put the follow-up date on your calendar.
6. *Prepare boss's mail.*
   Arrange mail in order of importance. Put urgent mail in red folder.
7. Attend to bills and statements according to the system used by your organization.

8. Attend to correspondence requiring your personal attention.
   Do it now!

Outgoing Mail

Use the same care with outgoing that you do with incoming mail.
After the letters have been signed and returned to you, check the
following:

Is the signature clear and clean? A smudged letter conveys a
poor impression.

Are the right enclosures in the right letter? If material is sent
under separate cover, make a note of it in the letter and send the
"separate cover" material the same day. Checks should be clipped
to the front of the letter near the letterhead.

If your office is not using computers or mail robots now, it probably will be soon. At Citibank in New York and at other companies,
robots deliver the mail, moving over the carpet from desk to desk.
Until that scary day when the computers take over the world, here
are a few tips to keep in mind:

Learn all you can about your executive's work so that you can
handle at least one-third of his correspondence, leaving only the
top-priority mail.

It's a good idea when you put urgent mail on your boss's desk not
to leave until it's been answered.

Keep a red folder for urgent mail, blue for important, and so on,
so mail doesn't get lost on a cluttered desk.

As we'll mention often, read every piece of correspondence that
comes across your desk. You learn, learn, learn that way—about
companies, about clients, and—most important—about your boss's
job. Get in the habit of underlining essential points.

Learn also about the special services offered by the U.S. Post
Office: aerograms, business reply mail, certificates of mailing,
CODs, overnight express mail, insured mail, mail grams, money
orders, passport applications, post-office boxes, registered mail,
self-serve postal centers, special delivery and special handling, and
Control Pak for maximum security mail such as credit cards. The
cards, placed in Control Pak plastic bags, are heat sealed against
theft, handled by the zip-code delivery supervisor, and delivered
by carrier.

FILING

No one likes to file. Ilona claims that in ten years she's never been asked for anything she's filed. The secret to not developing an overwhelming dislike for it is in our favorite maxim: Do it now! Simplify filing systems with ideas like color coding, cross-reference filing, C-file drawers. Maybe your company has switched to microfilm. Another suggestion: Put all the papers your boss needs on an imminent trip in a folder instead of in the files.

How to Set Up a Reminder File

"I forgot" are two words you shouldn't have to say. Correspondence, contracts, memos, reports, meetings, promises to keep, all the myriad details of your boss's and your life needn't worry you if you *keep a well-organized reminder file.*

You need only a file drawer and a set of file folders. Label 12 of the folders with the names of each month; label 31 with the numbers 1 through 31 (one for each day of the longest month) and label one "Future Years."

Put the daily folders in the front of the drawer in numerical order. Behind them, place the monthly folders, with next month's folder first and the current month's folder at the back. Place the folder marked "Future Years" at the extreme rear of the drawer.

Insert any follow-up material you now have in the folders according to when action must be taken or begun, either by filing the actual material directly into the reminder file or by using notes as a reminder and filing the actual material in the regular manner. If you put the material in the reminder file, be sure to note this in the regular file so you can find it if you need it.

Operating the Reminder File

Each morning remove the papers from that day's reminder file folder and transfer the empty folder to the rear of the file for the coming month. This way, you'll always have 31 folders for follow-ups—part of them for the remaining days of the current month and part of them for the beginning of the upcoming month.

Check the material. You'll find that much of the correspondence has already been answered. Destroy these copies or memos. Place material that's to be followed up more than 30 or 31 days later in the proper monthly folder, after labeling each paper with an exact follow-up date, if possible.

On the first of each month, transfer the material from that month's folder into the daily folders. Avoid filing material for follow-up on Saturdays, Sundays, and holidays by reversing the folders for those days.

Most of the above is predicated on the use of cabinets in which folders are arranged as alphabetically captioned guides, individual account folders, out guides, special name guides, and/or miscellaneous folders. There are also card cabinets for 3 × 5 cards, open-shelf storage, and the reminder file just discussed. You may also have microfilm storage.

Filing systems include:

Alphabetic—by subject, geography, or a combination of both.

Numeric—which includes the terminal-digit system popular with hospitals and insurance companies. The numbers are read right to left; the first and second numbers are the most significant, and the next two are secondary. For example, 78423 is read 23-84-7.

Phonetic—in which attention is on the sounds of the words. Police departments use this system when quick retrieval of information is important.

Active files are those you refer to once a month. Inactive files are seldom or never looked at and should be sent to central records. As for confidential material: Some phone numbers are private and should be kept out of sight. Keep all confidential material covered on your desk; many people can read upside down. Confidential files should be coded, and it's a good idea to put records or sensitive documents in a safe or give duplicates to a bank or attorney for safekeeping. Record disposal can mean putting material on microfilm or destroying it. Any destruction of classified material should be witnessed by the records administrator. Secretaries who type or take notes pertaining to classified material must shred, burn, or chemically decompose notes, carbon paper, scratch pads, and typewriter ribbons.

After you've worked for a while in an office that uses either centralized or decentralized filing systems, set up a method appropriate to your situation. Color code if possible, and teach your executive how to use the system to save time. Have charge-out forms available so you don't spend time tracking down lost material. Keep in mind the cost of processing a letter, which is said to be five dollars—inflation may have increased the cost by the time you read this—and encourage oral communication whenever feasible.

Finally, there's microfilm: Computer Output Microfilm (COM) picks up the data from the magnetic tapes and transfers them to a recorder by means of cathode-ray tubes that scan the page. A camera records the page onto microfilm and it ends as roll film, microfiche, or aperture cards. Hard copies can be made at any stage. This method of filing is economical and fast and takes up very little space. Microfilm, word processing, computers of all kinds are here to stay; their number will only increase in the office of the future.

We've been talking about filing as a technical skill: However, it has other aspects you might consider, such as keeping your own file on "who's who" and "what's what." Using index cards, you can keep track of the right person for the right job in your office, facts about your boss important for you to remember, the "unlisted" hierarchy of your organization—the Radars who get things done. If you work for an engineer or any other technical professional, jot down technical terms. Practice the vocabulary your boss employs. A legal secretary we know became indispensable because of the way she filed cases and the way she could retrieve them at a moment's notice. She was not only indispensable; she was promoted.

BASIC ACCOUNTING

As a secretary you'll probably do day-to-day record keeping for tax purposes. Maybe you'll need to know about employee stock option deductions, group insurance, savings bond purchases, and deductions. Depending on your office and the work it does, you might need some real estate and insurance fundamentals. An executive secretary should have a good working knowledge of stocks, bonds, and fixtures, plus an understanding of price earnings, ratios, and the financial pages of the newspaper. Could you interpret profit-and-loss statements? Do you know the meaning of debits, credits, liabilities, and so forth? Could you establish a petty cash fund?

We salute all secretaries who can pick through the maze of high finance, but for those of you who can't, but should be able to, we'll offer some basics. However, if your work depends on some knowledge of "the books," we suggest that you take a course or read one of the accounting texts recommended by your controller. If you work for a sales or manufacturing person and have a knack with numbers, sit in on meetings with accountants; that's a good way to get a feel for another field.

But let's start small, with the *petty cash fund*. What is it? Generally, it's a fund used for postage, carfare, or any item bought in small quantities. To start a fund, simply cash a check, and have some petty cash vouchers on hand for a record of who used it, how much was used, the date, and the receipt number. Vouchers are typically simple forms like the one in Figure 3. It's a good idea to put your boss's name on a slip if he borrows from the fund. Tell him about Harry Truman, who kept his own stamps in a drawer for his personal correspondence—or so the story goes. (They were three-cent stamps in those days.)

Many secretaries are in complete charge of the *payroll* and must have exact data on all employees and their salaries so they can maintain employee record cards like the one shown in Figure 4. What is a salary? Besides what there's never enough of, technically, a *salary* is compensation for someone who is paid for a month or longer and *wages* are payment for those paid by the hour, all at gross. Many firms now use computers to process payrolls, and it is a quick method. If your company is not using computers, it might be

Figure 3.   Petty cash voucher.

PETTY CASH VOUCHER

CHARGE TO:________________   ACCOUNT NO.:____________   DATE:__/__/__

AMOUNT:$______   AMOUNT:________________ DOLLARS   PAID BY:__________

FOR: ☐ STAMPS   ☐ TRAVEL & EXPENSE ADVANCE

☐ DINNER ALLOWANCE—ENTER DATES:__/__/__ __/__/__

☐ OTHER—PLEASE EXPLAIN __________________________

RECEIVED BY:________________   APPROVED BY:________________

Figure 4. Employee record card.

Name Address No. of Exemptions			Social Security No. Date of Birth Marital Status Hourly Rate Deductions								
EARNINGS											
Line No.	Week ended	Hours worked	Reg.	Over-time	Total	FICA	FWT	Total	Net	Ck. No.	Yr. to date
1 2											

using *punch cards* or *pegboard* systems. The all-too-familiar payroll deductions made by your employer are FICA (Social Security) and FWT (federal withholding tax). Some companies use time cards to record the information about employee's hours on a payroll register.

Which brings us to payroll taxes. If you maintain payroll records, in addition to name, address, Social Security number, amount and date of wage, withholding amount, identification number, and amount paid while employee is sick or injured, keep copies of statements relating to nonresident alien statutes. Also, if you work for a store, keep a record of the value and date of any noncash compensation paid to a retail salesperson from which no taxes were withheld.

Under the Federal Unemployment Tax Act, you need a record of:

- The total amount paid to employee in a calendar year.
- The amount of wages subject to unemployment tax and, if applicable, why the amount differs from the total compensation.
- The amount you paid into the state unemployment fund, showing deductions, nondeductions, and other data, depending on the type and size of your company.

Overall, there are three types of federal payroll taxes:

Income tax withheld
Social Security tax
Unemployment taxes

In addition, sounding like Japanese automobiles, are the FUTA and SUTA: federal unemployment and state unemployment tax, the employer's *payroll taxes.* If applicable, there is also *worker's compensation insurance.*

Typing tax returns is usually a secretary's responsibility. Often she keeps the records of her boss's income for tax purposes, even though the taxes will probably be paid by the accountant. Depending on the business, your company will pay property taxes or a sales tax in addition to income taxes (unless it's set up as a proprietorship or partnership). According to "step-by-step bookkeeping," if you are a secretary for a small business required to pay sales tax, you should enter the amount in the cash disbursements journal. The account is shown as "Sales Tax" and the amount is entered in the "Amount of Check" column and in the "Debit" column under general ledger items. The debit entry will later be posted to the "Sales Tax Payable" account in the general ledger. In the interest of simplification and to make life easier in a departmentalized store, the store should have all taxable items in one department and nontaxable items in another.

Now on to the almighty profit-and-loss (P&L) sheet. If there's been a profit, let's be sure it's recorded. Many times, the secretary has to assist in writing the financial report or income statement. It can be prepared monthly, quarterly, or semiannually, and simply put, it keeps a record of what comes in and what goes out. If you work for a manufacturer, include the cost of goods sold in addition to income or expenses. If you are helping to prepare a balance sheet, you must show (1) *assets*—owned by the business; (2) *liabilities*—owed by the business; and (3) *equity*—the difference between the two. A typical balance sheet is shown in Figure 5.

Secretaries are often in charge of the *expense account.* In private industry it's pretty straightforward, and a simple expense account form like that in Figure 6 is used, but in government, on all levels, it's complicated by bureaucracy. To be processed by the government, an expense account form must be signed by this chief and that chief and inspected by this head and that supervisor. By asking "why?" at each step, as we'll see when we talk about work simplification, we could undoubtedly eliminate many unnecessary steps in each piece of government correspondence. Saving steps is saving money—taxpayers' money. So if you're a government secretary, ask "why" when you take that expense account form around to be looked at, signed, initialed, and copied in triplicate.

THE BANK

For those of you who must balance checkbooks or take care of the money transactions in a small business, here are the steps to follow:

1. Put the checks in numerical order.
2. Compare the deposits in the checkbook with those on the statement and list deposits that are not in the statement.

Figure 5.   Typical balance sheet.

WIDGET COMPANY

ASSETS

Current Assets
1. Cash in bank
2. Accounts receivable
3. Petty cash
4. Supplies
5. Allowance for bad debts
6. Merchandise

Fixed Assets
1. Land
2. Buildings
3. Depreciation of buildings
4. Equipment
5. Depreciation of equipment
6. Improvements
7. Allowance for amortization

$32,000

LIABILITIES

Current
1. Accounts payable
2. Federal income tax withheld
3. State income tax payable

$8,000

CAPITAL

$24,000

Figure 6. Simple expense account form.

EXPENSE ACCOUNT FORM

Paid to: _________________ Name _________________

Purpose of trip: _________________________________

Dates: ____

Meals: ____

Travel: ____

Other: ____

Approved by: ____________________________________

Signature: ______________________________________

Date: ____

3. List outstanding checks and check off the cancelled checks.
4. Subtract service charges and the cancelled checks from deposits. Your balance should be the same as the bank's. If not—if there is some error—check with the bank immediately to see whether:
   a. Another company's check is posted to your account or vice versa.
   b. An amount is recorded incorrectly.
   c. An incorrect balance was forwarded from the preceding month.
   d. The computer in the bank made a mathematical error.

Banks offer many services, including:

Personal money orders (the same as personal checks) and cashier's checks.
Certified checks (a guarantee of payment).
Certificates of deposit (short-term interest).
Short-term checking accounts (just that).
Bank and sight and time drafts. (A bank draft is a check written by a bank on its money in another bank, a sight draft is a draft payable on presentation, and a time draft is a draft payable at a specified later time.)

If you're dealing with figures, in all probability you're using calculators, which are minicomputers. We assume that you have some familiarity with punch cards, microfilm, and word processing. Be prepared to need to become even more familiar with computers as time goes on. They're here to stay, and in ever-multiplying numbers.

BUSINESS WRITING TECHNIQUES

Business Letters

For an up-to-date business letter, use simplified, block, modified block, semiblock, or hanging indent letter styles. The date line, inside address, message, and signature block should conform in page placement. The secretary's initials should be placed double-spaced below the signature of the sender. A "cc" placed double-spaced below the secretary's initial indicates that carbon copies are being sent; it should be followed, of course, with the name(s) of the recipient(s). Paper should be of high quality, and typing should be neat. Any corrected errors should not be noticable. Today's ideal business language is clear and concise—no business jargon, please.

If you've been given the responsibility for composing letters, not just typing them, here are a few pointers. Taking for granted that you've consulted your boss on the procedures you are to follow regarding handling all correspondence and you know which letters you can handle directly, let's suppose that you're now ready to answer some of the mail.

- Collect everything you need.
- Note the important points in the letter being answered.
- Make an outline.
- If you are answering a letter, make margin notes on the letter before beginning the final draft.
- Write a clear opening sentence. Get the reader's interest.
- State the fundamental reason for your letter. Don't keep anyone guessing.
- Develop your letter from simple, factual sentences into logical paragraphs, using relevant examples.

- If writing an answer, be sure to speak to any questions that were raised.
- Use specific references to avoid misinterpretation.
- Summarize before closing.
- Proofread your letter carefully for typos and reread it for sense.
- Be friendly but not folksy.

A secretary's guide to writing some special correspondence is as follows:

Letter of Acknowledgment	Acknowledge the request and explain reason for the delay.
Letter of Inquiry	Detail the request. Mention due date.
Letter of Transmittal	Acknowledge interest in item. Give details on transmittal.
Letter of Adjustment	Acknowledge the error or complaint. Explain measures being taken to correct situation.
	Apologize and assure the customer it won't happen again.
	Offer appreciation for having the person as a customer and offer further service.
Sales Letter	Use a unique opening. Offer advantages of your product. See example, Figure 7.
Collection Letter	See example, Figure 8.

Here's a list of personal correspondence you might have to handle:

Appreciation	Response to invitations
Reservations	Introduction
Application	Condolences
Subscription	Congratulations

A word here about word processing. If your office does not have it yet, compose form letters, form paragraphs, and form thank you responses. They will soon come in handy.

Figure 7.   Sales letter.

Channel One/Dallas

Dear Friend:

I hope you know us. Our programs are as special as the people who watch them.

We need your support in order to maintain the outstanding quality of our programs.

Please keep Channel One number one by sending in your subscription today.

On behalf of a grateful television audience—thank you.

Sincerely,

R.J. Wing
President & General Manager

If you work for a government agency, special formats will be used, depending on whether or not the letter is classified, official, confidential, or top secret. Modified block lettering is generally used. The top and bottom are stamped according to one of the above classifications. No salutation or close is used. Write the author's title and surname and follow with the typist's initials in the upper right-hand corner. Use an inverted date on the date line and include the company's government contract number below the date. The name of the project comes next. Then type the subject flush left three lines below the date line. Below this is the line that starts with *To:* below that, *Through:* then *Reference:* and, at last, the message.

If you're a government secretary, be on the lookout for ways to streamline where you can. You're a taxpayer too.

If you make an error (and who hasn't?), admit it without excuses. Not only does it save time, but it is also so refreshing it might catch on. If your boss makes a mistake in a letter, you might ask "Don't

Figure 8. Collection letter.

MAINSTREET POTTERY

March 15, 1982

Mr. James Orwell
Orwell's Gifts
6 East McKinley Street
Deesville, Ohio 44660

Dear Mr. Orwell:

The terms of our wholesaling arrangement with you were that you would remit payment to us of $412.00 within thirty (30) days of receiving our shipment of pottery to your gift shop. Six weeks have gone by and we have yet to hear from you.

If your payment is already on the way to us, please disregard this letter. If you are having some difficulty, please let us know. We may be able to work out the problem.

Please let us hear from you soon.

Sincerely yours,

Kenneth Temple

adm

you think it would be better to say . . . ?" If he writes an angry, intemperate letter, wait until the storm blows over, then ask if he has reconsidered the whole thing before sending it off. Try if possible to get your boss to use a dictaphone, but if he *must* dictate, put up a "Do Not Disturb" sign while he's doing it.

A few notes about style: We've warned you against the overinflated language of Business Speak and will say more under "Memos." Just as important is to have a smooth flow in your communications. After you've eliminated all confusion from your letters, try to cut unnecessary words.

WRITE:	NOT . . .
The widgets can be shipped for $20.00.	at a cost of $20.00.
The shipment will be mailed later.	at a later date.
The shipment will be mailed from Texas.	from the state of Texas.
The shipment is in the warehouse until it can be shipped.	is at the present time in the warehouse until such time as it can be shipped to you.

USE:	NOT . . .
about	in reference to
at your request	in compliance with your request
separately	under separate cover
received	acknowledge receipt of
because	owing to the fact that

Cut where you can without sacrificing meaning. Use verbs instead of nouns when appropriate. Try "We adjusted the schedule" instead of "We made an adjustment in the schedule." It's stronger. Whenever possible, use positive language. Example: *Your Super Dooper Luscious Leather boots will give you long years of service when treated with our Waterproof Kit before wearing.*

Swallow hard and cut; persuade your boss that Business Speak slows down the pace, that pomposity isn't the same as importance.

Memos

What would any self-respecting office or business do without memos? A method of interoffice communication, they are frequently informal but must do what they set out to do—communicate. When they don't, time and energy are lost by the need for follow-up phone calls (phone calls might have done the job in the first place) or by additional memos seeking clarification of the original. So hold to the same principles of simplicity and clarity in memo writing as in letter writing.

Imagine if you will that a computer specialist has written a memo to all departments in a large organization about the newly installed terminal. Remember, she is not talking to *other* computer specialists.

> To: All Departments:
> From: Claire Keyes
> Subject: New Computer Terminal
>
> In order that we may maximize our utilization of the new computer terminal, we will seminar all day Monday in Conference Room A at 9:00 A.M. to familiarize all departments with the new facility. Please finalize all programs prioritized by your department and bring them with you to the meeting for group feedback. Remember, the output from this seminar will be only as good as your input. Let's all become computer wise.

Has Claire been clear? Or has she instead created a fat, over-dressed memo? Is a thin, tailored message buried in there trying to get out? What if Claire sent the following:

> To: All Departments
> From: Claire Keyes
> Re: New Computer Terminal
>
> On Monday there will be an all-day seminar in Conference Room A (9:00 A.M.) on the maximum use of the computer terminal. Please bring your top priority programs for review.

Remember that old school exercise of compare and contrast? The most obvious contrast, of course, is length; the second memo is clearly much shorter. But brevity for the sake of brevity isn't a virtue. Does the shorter memo relay all the pertinent information its recipients need? Well, it tells when, Monday (9:00 A.M.); what, an all-day seminar; where, Conference Room A; why, to discuss how best to use the new computer terminal; and gives directions to those attending: Bring your programs for review. Is that all the participants must know? That's really all Claire told them in the first memo.

News Releases

News writing requires its own kind of pacing. On the chance that you might be asked to write a news release one day, aim for giving the facts as briefly as possible. But you must be both brief *and* factual. A famous humorist once had a career as a newspaper man. Sent to cover a murder, he wrote the lead (the opening paragraph—one sentence in most papers) and gave the completed story to his editor, only to be told that the lead was too long. After many unsuccessful attempts at rewriting, he returned with his final effort. It read: "Dead, he was." Brief, it is, but it only has one fact.

Brevity in the lead is dear to the hearts of most editors and journalism teachers. One professor holds his students to 25-word leads; 30 words seem to be average in most metropolitan papers. But the lead's function is to give you the heart of the story. In other words, news stories operate on the inverted pyramid principle: The significant facts are given first (not in chronological order) and everything follows in descending order of importance. Since space is always a factor, the idea is that if you must cut, you can chop from the bottom and not lose the central facts. So, remember, who, what, when, where, and—if possible—why or how are all given up front.

If, for example, you are called on to send in an announcement of a new appointment in your organization, it could go like this:

> The Obscure Widget Company announced today the appointment of Leslie Winner as vice-president of research and development, effective immediately. Dr. Winner, formerly on the faculty of the University of Chicago, brings a strong theoretical background in widgetry to her new post, according to company president, Craig Curtis.
>
> "We expect that Dr. Winner, combining as she does both a practical and a theoretical knowledge of widgetry,

> will help put the Obscure Widget Company on the map, both nationally and internationally," Curtis said.
>
> A graduate of the University of Michigan, Professor Winner earned her doctorate at the University of Wisconsin. She spent five years with Widgets, Inc., before returning to the academic world. Professor Winner succeeds T. M. Marshall, who has retired after long service with Obscure.

The lead could also be written this way: "The Obscure Widget Company announced today that University of Chicago professor Dr. Leslie Winner has been named vice-president of research and development, effective immediately." Additional biographical details about the appointee or facts about the company would follow.

An example of the use of proofreading marks, which can be found in many dictionaries, is given in Figure 9.

Reports

The formal report has the following parts:

Cover—listing the title and author
Fly leaf—a blank page
Title fly—the title
Title page—title and subtitle, department, firm name, address, and date
Authorization and transmittal letters—purpose of report
Acknowledgments—those who assisted
Table of contents
List of illustrations
Synopsis—a summary
Report body—introduction, purpose, and conclusions
Footnotes
Appendix
Bibliography
Index

If you have helped write the report, make certain that you receive acknowledgment; after more exposure to your boss's projects and work, you may eventually write the reports by yourself. For

Figure 9.   Example of proofread copy.

¶ Some organizations produce in-house Newsletters that are
concerned with the employee news, often of a personal
nature--engagements, weddings, children's graduations, re-
tirements, and so on. The secretary may become involved in
putting them together.

     If the format calls for ② or more columns, type a draft
first. And proofread everything you write or type from memos,
letters, news releases, reports, and newsletter/house organs.
we suggest reading backwards, because the eye than sees the
words objectively. Copy marking in general use may be found
in most desk reference manuals and dictionaries.

this to happen, you'll need some knowledge of the company. Research any facts you might need, especially those of a technical
nature. Take advantage of company files, your company's library,
or the public library and the expertise of the research librarian. If
you use footnotes, include the author's name, title of publication,
editor, edition, volume number, geographical location of publisher, publisher's name, publication date, and page number. A
bibliography contains the same information as a footnote, but it is
arranged alphabetically by author last names.

There are also *letter reports* written for groups outside the company; *short business reports,* informally written; and *memorandum reports,* which are routine and are written for in-house use.

4

Administrative Skills

In some places there's a cult of busyness, of activity for its own sake. We hope to show that adequate planning produces results, the central reason for activity. It isn't how much you do but what you get done that matters. Do meetings matter?

MEETINGS

Setting up a Meeting

Sometimes we wonder if one person's meeting is not another person's coffee break with co-workers. Meetings in many companies proliferate like memos, and it's often up to you to set them up, invite the participants, attend, take minutes, write the minutes, and submit a report. With a thorough knowledge of the company and your boss's job, someday you may also run the whole thing yourself. But first, let's get the people to the meeting, whether it's a regularly scheduled one, a special executive session, an annual stockholders' meeting, a corporate directors' meeting, or a conference.

Invitations

An interoffice memo will suffice as a reminder for a regular meeting. For a board of directors meeting, send out an announcement something like the one shown in Figure 10.

Figure 10.   Announcement for board of directors meeting.

BOARD OF DIRECTORS MEETING

Chairperson: _______________________________________

Date: ____

Place: ____

Board Members:

_______________________   _______________________

_______________________   _______________________

_______________________   _______________________

Total to Attend: ___________________________________

Regular: ____

Special: ____

Guaranteed Attendance: _____________________________

At board of directors meetings you must include the board's report, appointments, nominations, and elections. At a stockholders meeting, take along the corporate seal, a copy of the corporate laws, the certificate of incorporation, the current meeting file, and the minute books. For an informal meeting, simply make the introductions and start the discussions. Remain impartial.

Nothing substitutes for planning. Make arrangements well in advance and do a follow-up at the end. Keep a checklist handy. (See management-by-objective exercises in Chapter 8 to see how one secretary worked out arrangements for a large conference that became a prototype for future meetings of that scale.) See Figure 11 for an example of a meeting checklist and Figure 12 for an example of a schedule for a large meeting.

A *social event* may require an RSVP. Decide first when, where, how many rooms, for how long, and how many. Then notify the caterer. Send a reservation postcard for an outside business meeting, and put a notice in the company's newsletter. After everybody has been notified, decide which seating arrangement is best, ac-

Figure 11. Daily conference/convention checklist.

To: Catering Manager
From: Andi Bardan
Administrative Secretary
Date: March 21, 19___

Type of Meeting: Management Skills for Government Secretaries
Place of Meeting: Grand Hotel, Washington, D.C.
Meeting Dates: March 21–23, 19___

Date	Time	A.M.	P.M.	Room	Function	Room Setup	Number of Guests	Menus A/V Equipment
3/21	9–12	A.M.		Polynesian	Management-by-Objective Exercises	Team Tables for 35	35	1 Lectern 1 Film Projector, 16 mm 1 Video Tape Mach.
	10–10:15	A.M.		Caribbean	Coffee Break	Self-Service Tables	35	Coffee Fruit
	12:15–1:15		P.M.	Aruba	Lunch	Five Tables for Seven People Each	35	Consommé Baked Sesame Chicken Green Salad Rolls Lemon Tart Coffee/Tea
	1:30–4:30		P.M.	Polynesian	Time Management	Same as 9–12	35	Same as 9–12
	3–3:15		P.M.	Caribbean	Coffee Break	Self-Service	35	Coffee Cheese Assorted Crackers

cording to the size of the group—panel formation; round table; U, L, or T formation; teams; or schoolroom style. These days it's advisable to have smoking and nonsmoking areas. For a meeting outside the company, prepare an agenda and itinerary for each participant's folder, plus information on translation and secretarial services, doctors, entertainment, restaurants, and transportation. You may be required to arrange tours for accompanying spouses. Be sure to see to all audiovisual needs, such as chalkboards (and chalk, of course) flip charts, lecterns, pencils, markers, projectors, and recorders.

As for food, why not break the coffee and sweet roll habit? The sweet rolls are usually more pasty than pastry and are always fattening. Have the coffee in the morning for those who can't start without it, but try fruit and cheese at the breaks. Protein is a longer-lasting source of energy than carbohydrates. Check if any special diet requirements must be met. You may have some vegetarians in the group. Keep the air flowing and the temperatures comfortable (on the coolish side, but we could get some argument about that) and for those who insist on smoking, see that no overflowing ashtrays are left to foul the air.

On the day of the meeting, when all the amenities have been completed, greet the participants, see that they register, give them badges (if used), and inform them where they can receive phone messages. Placecards, folders, pens, and pencils should be at each place.

Minutes

Keep minutes short and to the point. Include the date of the meeting, location, time of day, name of presiding officer, kind of meeting, names of those present, and, for larger groups, a quorum check. Next state the order of the business conducted and the motions that were made. Before you write reports of any meeting, understand what the meeting was all about, the business discussed, and all the other particulars. It's a good way to gain recognition for yourself. Before long you may preside at meetings and be able to delegate the planning to others.

Figure 12.   Example of schedule for large meeting, such as a seminar.

**ASSERTIVENESS TRAINING
FOR EXECUTIVE SECRETARIES AND
ADMINISTRATIVE ASSISTANTS**

Neuse Hotel, Denver, Colorado: December 1–3, 1980

Course Leader: Joyce Lively, Consultant
Peachtree Plaza, Atlanta, Ga.

Monday, December 1, 1980   **Speaker**

9:00–9:30	Registration	
9:30–9:45	Opening Remarks	
9:45–10:30	Registrant Introduction	
10:30–11:15	*Presentation and Group Discussion* A Re-View of the Woman's Role	Course Leader
11:15–11:45	*Film Presentation* Pack Your Own Chute	Course Leader
11:45–12:30	*Participative Exercises Relating To Film and Focus of Morning Presentation*	Course Leader
12:30–1:30	Lunch	
1:30–3:00	*Social Milieu and the Role of the Secretary*	Course Leader
3:00–5:00	*Presentation and Participative Exercises*	Course Leader

Tuesday, December 2, 1980

9:00–10:30	*Presentation and Participative Exercises* Assertive Responses for Secretaries	Course Leader
10:30–10:45	Coffee Break	
10:45–12:30	*Presentation and Group Discussion* The Secretary Gains Respect	Course Leader
12:30–1:30	Lunch	
1:30–2:30	*Presentation and Participative Exercises* Working with Your Boss for Recognition	Course Leader
2:30–2:45	Coffee Break	
2:45–5:00	*Presentation and Participative Exercises* Working with Peers	Course Leader

Wednesday, December 3, 1980   **Speaker**

9:00–11:15	*Presentation and Participative Exercises* Examining Assertive Goals	Course Leader
11:15–11:30	Coffee Break	
11:30–12:30	*Presentation and Group Discussion* Personal and Professional Goals	Course Leader
12:30–1:30	Lunch	
1:30–2:30	*Project Session* Workshop for Executive Secretaries and Administrative Assistants (Goal-Setting Workshop)	
2:30–3:00	Large Group Discussion and Sharing Workshop Results	
3:00–3:30	Summary and Closing Remarks	

Chairing a Meeting

Chairing a meeting is not as frightening as it seems because there is a procedure to follow—Robert's Rules of Order for formal meetings:

Call to order	Committee reports
Roll call	Unfinished business
Minutes of previous meetings	New business
Reading of correspondence	Programs
Treasurer's report	Arrangements
Officers' reports	Adjournment

TRIPS

If you communicate well with your boss, you'll learn his travel preferences. With good planning, you'll be able to set up a trip like a one-person travel agency. You'll become familiar with guides, travel agency services, hotels that your boss likes, and hotels that are reasonably priced. Be a stickler for the details of reservations and confirmations. Save time by using a travel agency. If your boss often uses the same airline, write a bunch of tickets yourself. The airline charges the number to your company. Cancel the ones you don't use.

Preparing an itinerary is very important. See Figure 13 for a sample itinerary. As soon as you know about a pending trip, start assembling in a folder all the materials that will be required: contracts, speeches, formats for meetings, reading material, and any other papers your boss will need, all labeled with special instructions, giving the particulars of time, place, and so forth. It's also a good idea to attach a checklist of those items that are always included on a trip for the day you may not be there. Figure 14 offers a sample trip checklist.

As that one-person travel agency, make certain your boss has the necessary vaccinations, passports, and visas for any overseas trip. You can get a detailed pamphlet on customs regulations from a district director of customs located in various cities. Write to the area director of customs in New York, NY 10004; in Washington, DC 20018; in Chicago, IL 6060; in Anchorage, AK 99501; in Houston, TX 77052; in Savannah, GA 31401; in Boston, MA 02109; in Los Angeles, CA 90052; or in San Pedro, CA 90731.

Acceptable and nonacceptable behavior varies greatly in different countries. In strict Muslim countries such as Kuwait and Saudi Arabia, for instance, religious practice forbids alcohol. In Japan much business is conducted at clubs or restaurants. Generally speaking, in most countries (America seems to be an exception), it's an honor to be asked into a person's home and invitations are infrequent. But if you are invited to a private home, the occasion will be considered strictly social. Suggest that your boss brush up on theater, music, and the arts. In Jordan it's proper to bring the host, not the hostess, a gift.

If your boss is a woman, urge her not to wear pants suits when traveling on business. For male executives, dark, conservative suits usually are safe, but tell them to avoid "rep" or club ties in London. It's considered bad form to wear "imitations" of one of theirs.

It's generally best to make appointments beforehand. Have calling cards printed up to pass around.

British Airways puts out a book called *The Golden Guide* that includes city briefings: information on taxis, flights, car hires, holidays, dentists, doctors, and chemists (druggists), plus conference advice, names of hairdressers, hotels, restaurants, bars, shops, and concert halls. If you're not going along, your boss can also find

Figure 13.   Sample itinerary.

ITINERARY: R.C. Wheeler
A.D. James

Monday, January 19:
Chauffeur will pick you up at your home at 6:45 A.M.

Cleveland/Mexico   AA #93   Depart: 8:15 A.M.
  City   (1 stop: Dallas) Arrive: 1:00 P.M.
(Coach)

Portillo to meet flight and arrange for you to travel to San Luis Potosí and stay at a halfway house for the night.

Tuesday, January 20:
Return to Mexico City from San Luis Potosí

Hotel reservations for January 20–23 at:
Hotel el Presidente
Campos 812   Phone: (905) 555-4567
Mexico 5, D.F. Mexico   Telex: 001-1000

Wednesday, January 21:
Board of directors meeting

Friday, January 23:
Mexico City/Atlanta   EA #908   Depart: 9:15 A.M.
(Coach)   (nonstop)   Arrive: 1:17 P.M.

Atlanta/Cleveland   Delta #1640 Depart: 4:14 P.M.
(Coach)   (nonstop)   Arrive: 5:50 P.M.

Chauffeur will meet your flight and take you home.

secretarial services in the guide. We will give you some names and addresses for overseas secretarial services here:

SECRETARIAL SERVICES

Amsterdam   International Sec. N.V.
c/o Rotterdam Hilton Hotel
Weena 10, Rotherdam
Tel: 010-120772
010-148988

Nederlands, Genootschap van
Vertalas Van Nijenrodeweg 69
Tel: 44 67 96

Athens

Exec. Services
Athens Tower Suite 506
Building B
Tel: 77 83 698, Telex: 21-4227

Venetsianou Antigoni
Macedonon Street 2
Tel: 64 65 987

Berlin

Congress Service Berlin
Sybelstrasse 44
Tel: 885 14 67

Copenhagen

Hovedbanegardens Oversaet-
 telses
Bureau, Central Station
Tel: 129736
(central railway system—typing,
 duplicating)

Frankfurt

Stolze-Schrey
Schumannstrasse 67
Tel: 77 2883

Geneva

Erka Office
81 Avenue Louis Casal
Tel: 348360
(multilingual—fully equipped
 exec. offices for hire daily)

Manpower
6 Rue Winkelried
Tel: 31 6800
(multilingual, including
 weekends and evenings)

Sec. Services
2 Rue des Voisins
Tel: 298027

London

Forum
15-16 New Burlington St., W.I.
Tel: 01-493-1351
(multilingual)

T.I.P.S.
310 Regent St. WI
Tel: 01-580-7011
(24 hr. service)

Madrid

Steno Services
Alberto, Alcocer 10
Tel: 457 71 55

Milan

International Bus. Centre
Corso Vittorio Emanuele 15
Tel: 749 0009

Interpreters and Translators

Paris

Bis
120 Boulevard Diderot
Tel: 344 7613

Europe Secretariat
27 Rue du Septembre
Tel: 742-0989

Euro Traduction
54 Avenue Charles de Gaulle
Tel: 747-8574

Inter Domes
15 Avenue de l'Opera
Tel: 260 30 58

Manpower
88 Rue Lafayette
Tel: 770 73 69

Rome

Barberini Agency
Barberini, Largo Torriolo 20
Tel: 4894 11

International Sec. Agency
Argo Torriolo 20
Tel: 56 4692

Vienna

Sekretarian aut Abruf
Wickenburggasse 22
Tel: 4316 16

Some hotels also provide secretarial services.

It's also advisable to register any cameras, tape recorders, or other articles that can be identified by a serial number. Suggest also that in the interest of time and convenience only carry-on luggage be used. Your company's bank will set up a line of credit through a letter of credit if your boss needs money in another country. Check that he has traveler's checks. Foreign currency can be purchased at a bank. But no matter what arrangements are made, you may still be called on to send an express money order in a hurry.

Figure 14.   Sample trip checklist.

TRIP CHECKLIST

Itinerary: flights, hotels, meetings, who will meet him.
Passports and visas when required.
Health card.
Money in traveler's checks.
Tickets.
Business cards.
Letter from company stating that your boss is traveling on its
    behalf.
Any medication needed. Check that supply is adequate.
Addresses and phone numbers of the people boss is seeing.
Home and home office phone numbers of key office per-
    sonnel.
Hotel confirmation slips.
Papers and reading material for meetings.
Summary of weather conditions.
Paperbacks for pleasure reading.
Clothes sizes of family or friends for whom boss might want to
    buy gifts.

We've been assuming that you'll be tending the office fires while your boss is winging here and there but occasionally you may be asked to go along. If you work for a woman, there's no problem. (Of course, you could be a male secretary. . . .) Actually, there's really no problem anyway if you're always professional. So stay in the same hotel; it's more convenient if you have to work late. Dine together occasionally when it seems only appropriate and human to do so.

And now for a final, rather sneaky, suggestion. If your boss returns on the 23rd, for example, tell everybody that he won't be back in the office till the 24th. It's a chance to clear up his urgent correspondence and other matters that need his attention. You could also tell people he's leaving the day before he actually goes so that you both have a chance to take care of last-minute details.

TIME MANAGEMENT

All those trips, all those meetings, reports to get out, letters to write, deadlines to meet, fires to fight. And the endless lament of not enough time. But the paradox is, as we read somewhere, that "We never have enough time, yet we have all the time there is." And many of us are chronic time strugglers, afflicted with a sense of time urgency.

The time struggler is often thought to be an executive or chairman of the board or president of a major business, but time urgency can afflict anybody, from florist to pharmacist, stevedore to secretary. Do you have that sense of urgency? Or perhaps you suffer from the related problem of procrastination. Is there an answer? Well, one way may be to cease struggling with time and learn how to manage it instead—take charge of your time.

Cardiologists Meyer Friedman and Ray Rosenman suggest pasting on your bathroom mirror or on the one in your office desk a reminder that "Life is an unfinishedness." (Procrastinators know that in a different sense.) In other words, do each day what you (realistically) planned (and plan each working day). Know that the unexpected will often (always?) upset those plans, so stay flexible; and then put that day behind you.

In this chapter we'll offer some suggestions from Alan Lakein, the time management consultant, and some practical ideas from secretaries to put you in control of the clock. We hope they will be a jumping-off place for ideas of your own: Only you know your own days, working conditions, and temperament. Time management is really only common sense; a seemingly simplistic system, a kind of "what's the big deal?" method. All true, but it's easy to backslide; your commitment to organizing your time should be renewed periodically or the same old "hurry sickness" will lay you low gain.

Lakein offers these proposals as a starting point: A secretary and her boss should (1) be a team, (2) communicate, (3) be organized. His organizational methods, famous by now, are as follows:

1. List goals and set priorities.
2. Make a daily "To Do" list.
3. Start with As, not Cs (A means top priority, urgent; B has to be done but not now; and C can probably be put off forever).
4. Ask yourself if this is the best use of your time right now.
5. Handle a piece of paper only once (seems impossible but we will elaborate on this idea).
6. Do it now!

On a piece of paper, list your goals, putting an A, B, or C after each. Keep in mind that the average person spends 80 percent of his or her time doing the things that are in the lowest 20 percent of importance and 20 percent of the time doing what brings 80 percent of the rewards. As Friedman and Rosenman suggest: "Stop using your right hand to do the work your left hand should be doing."

Look over your list and make the Bs either As or Cs. If by now your A list is huge, don't wait until you can do it all at once—you'll never find the time. Start by biting off small pieces; say, in the 10 minutes you have before lunch. Don't scorn those small amounts of time. You can wear away a mountain that way. But whatever you do with those odd amounts of time, don't do a C.

Each day make a daily "To Do" list to bring your A mountain down to size. Again, be sure it's a reasonable list so that at the end of the day you can cross off what you've accomplished. That's the pleasure of lists.

Handle a piece of paper only once. It may seem impossible, but it works. Constantly shifting piles of paper, reading material, and so on because you think you'll get to them later only makes them grow. You shift them again, stacking neatly each time, and the paper mountain is larger still. Maybe you even take papers home and bring them back again. You *can* make that mountain a molehill. Even if you only write on the upper right-hand corner of the page "see Jones," do something with each piece of paper you handle. And throw away right away what needs to be junked.

Only you can do it now, so do it now! An old proverb has it that "One of these days is none of these days." It's also interesting to discover that what you do now takes less time than what you do later. It's another of Murphy's Laws: A task grows in proportion to the length of time you put off doing it.

Ask yourself, "What's the best use of my time right now?" It may be thinking, or planning, or quietly recharging, or taking a break. In another context, it can mean using each minute wisely. If you must wait for your boss, for instance, bring other work to do, plan your next project, or do some pertinent reading, but don't just stew impatiently.

What are your time wasters? Here's a list of common ones compiled by secretaries. Check those that apply to you, add your own, and write down your ideas for controlling them. Do it now!

Telephones	Inability to say no to other managers
Drop-in visitors	
Correspondence	Lack of objectives, deadline pressure
Typing	
Dictation	Meetings scheduled or unscheduled
Filing	
Reading	Boss and secretary's calendars not coordinated
Socializing, idle conversation	Failure to do first things first
Personal errands for boss	Leaving tasks unfinished or jumping from one task to another and attempting too much at once
Constantly switching priorities	
Poor communication	

Waiting	Crises, emergencies, fire fighting
Copy machines	
Procrastination, indecision	Cluttered desk or office, personal disorganization

Here is an action plan for controlling your top time wasters.

Switching Priorities

Since you and your boss are a team, get together each morning to discuss priorities even if you can manage only three minutes. Both of you should be playing the same game, so that you don't have to keep switching priorities. Try to consolidate interruptions by scheduling them at quarter to the hour.

Crisis Deadlines

1. Ask supervisor first thing each morning what plans are for the day and begin collecting the necessary data.
2. Ask supervisor to inform you of regularly scheduled deadlines so that you may remind him well in advance and/or collect the necessary information.
3. Ask questions 1 and 2 of others in the office for whom you're required to do some work.
4. Ask all in the office who give you work to indicate on the task what the deadline is. You can schedule the really "hot" ones first.
5. If your office is in a constant panic, there could be something wrong with the way it's managed. Have a meeting with other secretaries in the department on how to solve the problem. Then go as a group to the department head, solutions in hand, and ask for help.
6. Use Word Processing whenever possible.
7. If someone is writing a lengthy document that will need typing, ask him or her to give it to you as it's written. It's better than for you to be expected to have the whole thing typed in ten minutes.

Establishing Priorities with Multiple Bosses

1. Establish a chain of command.
   a. Boss is first (who is boss?).
   b. Establish importance of others (or their projects) with boss.
2. Determine the deadline for the job—now, in an hour? Propose a time when the job might be completed and let the giver decide if that will do or the job should be given to someone else.
3. Establish a backup work relationship with fellow clerical people in the department so that work can be referred to them if necessary.
4. Set aside a time each day to do routine things that must be completed daily, such as opening the mail.
5. Convince yourself that you have the option to refuse to take on another task if you absolutely cannot get to it. Nobody functions effectively with the weight of the world on her shoulders.
6. Do work on a first-come, first-served basis.
7. If everything is defined as top priority, have all the bosses get together and decide on the true top priority. It's their decision.
8. Post a daily "things to do" sheet where everyone can see it.

An Unorganized Boss

1. Ask him what you might do to help. If he has no answers, offer helpful suggestions.
2. Implement the solutions on which you both agree. Some of these may be:
   a. Set up a logging system for papers entering and leaving his office. You can ask for them if they don't reappear soon.
   b. Set up a colored-folder system for correspondence needing his attention. For example, you might make a yellow folder for letters that need his signature; a red folder for items needing immediate action; and a blue folder for things that can be read at leisure.
   c. Insist on a few minutes each day to inform each other of the day's activities and problem areas.

   d. Establish a checkout system for your files. Insert a checkout card when he wants a file; then you'll know he has it. If you don't get it back in a few days, ask for it.

   e. Assert yourself about needing to know his whereabouts when he leaves the office.

   f. Organize his desk each morning or afternoon so that you'll know what's being worked on.

   g. Screen telephone callers and help those you can or refer them to someone who can, if possible.

   h. Avoid interrupting meetings, but establish what interruptions are acceptable.

   i. Use brightly colored cards on his desk for appointment reminders. These will stand out from all the white papers already on the desk.

A Co-worker Who Is Reluctant to Help Out

1. Specifically ask the problem co-worker for assistance.
2. Hold group sessions with all secretaries in the department to discuss the problem, including the "problem child."
3. Designate a "workload manager" for the department to distribute work during peak periods.
4. Always thank those who help and tell their supervisors about their contributions.
5. Barter. Offer assistance when the problem worker is overloaded in return for her help now.

Jumping from One Task to Another

Remember, start with an A, not a C; even, we repeat, if you can only do part of the task. Avoid the tendency to jump from one task to another, finishing nothing.

"I'd Rather Do It Myself"

Don't be like the mother who always cleans her children's rooms because it's easier for her to do it herself. As a result, her children never learn how to do for themselves. If you have work that can be delegated, spend time now training other secretaries in the work; you'll save time later.

Emergencies

Schedule one hour a day for fire fighting and problem solving.

Copying

Copying machines are a recurrent problem for many secretaries. It might help to:

Maintain a daily record of each employee's use of the machine.
Compute a daily average.
Classify each employee's usage as active, inactive, or very active.
Put up schedules.

Copy once a day, if possible. You might also compute how many hours are wasted in waiting for the machine and in the copying process itself. On the principle that time equals money, maybe it would pay the company to hire someone specifically for that job. It would also cut down the clutter found by many copy machines.

We recognize this as a major headache for many secretaries. The scenario goes something like this at many places: The duplicating department is perceived as uncooperative and uninterested in doing a good job. Material is returned, secretaries claim, dirty, incomplete, and out of order. To avoid that, secretaries try to do big jobs on floor copiers, overloading or misusing them. The result is frequent breakdowns. Outside repairmen are then called in and while the secretaries are waiting, they rush to other floors to use other copiers, thus overloading and misusing them.

Some organizations have hired a specific person to do the copy work normally done by the secretaries and to act as key operators; that is, make all paper changes, load and unload paper, handle the disposition of any breakdowns, and do similar chores. In addition to the regular floor machines, several desk copiers (there are some fine American-made ones) are used to ease the load on the major machines.

A record of activity summary for other equipment use can also be useful, and may be set up in a mode similar to that for copy machine records.

A Cluttered Desk

If you can function in clutter, okay. For justification we cite the slogan, "A cluttered desk is the mark of genius," but mostly, clutter's just the mark of disorder. Searching for things is an enormous waste of time, so if you can't work in clutter, separate the minimum and maximum work areas. Try an equipment checklist:

- Are there proper storage facilities?
- Are files of right type for their use?
- Have special commercial files been considered for special needs?
- Are machines of right type (electric or hand, rotary or key driven, printing calculator)?
- Are they being used properly?
- How much are machines used daily? Are there enough or too many? Should they be used at all?
- Can single-pedestal desks be used instead of standard sizes?
- Are comptometer desks provided for operators?
- Are posture chairs in use? If not, should they be provided?
- Are the amount and kind of telephone equipment adequate?
- Is a buzzer system needed?
- Are desks at the proper height for the individual?
- Can equipment be specially designed for the job (sorting board, stamp rack, posting tray, ledger support, filing tray)?

Procrastination

"We have met the enemy and they is us," Pogo announced. Another sage, quoted constantly, proclaimed procrastination to be the thief of time. Do it now!

Visitors

Even if your boss has an open-door policy, compromise and arrange for the staff to come at certain times of the day. An open-door policy doesn't need to be applied literally. Also, recommend that your boss meet people in the waiting room or stay on his feet when visitors come in.

Typing

Use a dictaphone. Your boss can dictate and you can type when it's convenient for you both. If the boss complains that a dictaphone is too impersonal, you can always put your picture (or somebody else's) in front of the machine. Word Processing (more later) is here to stay.

Dictation

If your boss must dictate (and according to some bosses, there are times when it's appropriate), suggest to the draft-happy type that he make an outline and let you compose the letter. If a letter is urgent, stand there until he answers it.

Saying No

Your boss's work is your top priority. It's your job, what you're paid to do. You may say no to other managers' work requests. (See the Assertiveness section in Chapter 6.)

Personal Errands

This is a thorny, symbolic issue to many secretaries. If you want to bring coffee to your boss or perform other personal errands, it's up to you. If you don't, it would help your position if your responsibilities were spelled out in a job description. Read more on this subject in Chapter 6.

Lack of Objectives

Again, coordinate with your boss. Discuss your responsibilities and objectives. List goals with time frames, as discussed in detail in Chapter 8.

Meetings

Get material ready at least one week ahead of any prescheduled meeting.

Communication

Try paraphrasing what your boss tells you to make certain you've understood. Have anyone you may supervise restate what you tell them.

Calendars

Check that your calendar and your boss's read the same.

Time Log

It's essential to record the way you actually spend your time (as opposed to how you think you spend it) every so often to find ways of using it to better advantage.

Reports

A well-designed form can cut the preparation time of a report in half. If the report is already filled in on a form, perhaps you can improve the design.

Interruptions

We know of one large company with a unique time-saving rule: Between 8:30 and 9:30 A.M. *no* interruptions are permitted. This applies without exception to all employees. You'd be surprised how much work gets done.

Socializing

Take the chair away from your desk. One secretary did and reports it worked wonders. Tell potential visitors that you'll meet them at coffee break, but you're busy now. Explain to the intruder that you're fighting a deadline and will call her when you're finished.

If a group gathers around, say rather loudly, but with good humor, "Please folks, I can't hear myself think," or perhaps something wittier. Explain that: "My boss does not like me to spend much time socializing when I should be working." If all of the above fail, politely ask them to move on.

Reading

Try speed-reading and scanning. Read the first and last chapters to determine the essence of what you're studying. Note everything that's underlined. News articles run from the most important to the least significant. But speed-reading is not for *War and Peace:* "I read it in 15 minutes," Woody Allen claims. "It's about Russia."

Boss's Time Problems

Sometimes no matter how you save your boss's time, time wasters put you right back to ground eero. Here's a list of the top ten time wasters compiled by more than 50 chairmen, presidents, and vice-presidents:

Phone
Mail
Meetings
Public relations
Paperwork
Commuting
Business lunches
Civic duties
Incompetents
Family demands (when asked to elucidate, they said "no comment").

Some experts not only stress the need for long- and short-range planning and strict deadlines for secretaries, managers, and executives, but also recommend the stand-up meeting we mentioned before. There's even an unnerving Danish device called an econometer that ticks away the time, revealing the rising cost of a meeting computed from the hourly pay of those present.

Other experts advise managers to move quickly on reversible decisions (organization changes), but more slowly on irreversible ones (firings); to handle problems one at a time but begin actions on them concurrently; and to make the best use of time for the highest return.

All that might be true, but the greatest time-saver of them all is a superefficient secretary, and most businessmen concede that. "The ideal secretary is an obsessive-compulsive . . . who gets hives when she sees your desk is messy and won't let you leave the office without an idiot card that tells you where you're going, who you're going to meet, and what's going to be discussed," says Dreyfus Corporation President Jerome Hardy.

"A good secretary," he adds, "gives you the gift of time." She's often a source of untapped ideas as well. Since time is money and the efficient secretary is an acknowledged time-saver, we'd like to see her receive not a *gift,* but what she's entitled to: recognition for her worth.

Many woman nowadays combine two time-consuming careers. A national survey found that women who work full time also do more than 80 percent of the household chores. Basic management principles—planning, organizing, controlling, and delegating—are applicable both at home and in the office.

WORK SIMPLIFICATION

Would that you could squirrel away your time, securing it against all those days with not enough hours in them, but you can't accumulate your minutes in a bank. You can only use them to get done what you want to get done. Work simplification is one way to get things done in the most efficient way, by "working smarter, not harder."

Work simplification can be defined as: (1) doing only the things necessary to get the work done; (2) eliminating all unnecessary details; and (3) combining steps whenever possible by rearranging the sequence of operations. It aims to improve ways of doing the necessary things while eliminating the unnecessary.

According to Sir Henry Deterding, head of the Royal Dutch

Shell Company, ". . . everything that is complicated is wrong. Simplicity rules everything that is worthwhile."

Find out what makes things tick. Take procedures apart and see how they function, see what can be improved, and above all ask why things are done that way. Don't accept "Because they've always been done that way" or "That's just the way we do things around here." Find out why. We're sure you'll find ways to improve or simplify procedures and along the way discover more interesting things about your work. The more you know about something, the more control you have over it and the more it becomes yours.

Let's simplify work simplification. You need to use work distribution charts, process flow charts, and work count. List all the activities on the left-hand side of a work distribution chart. Put the person's initials at the top and under the initials the various tasks that person performs in relation to that activity. Put the hours in the column on the right-hand side (see Figure 15).

Next, take a piece of paper and follow the process through the different steps by using symbols (Figure 16 to 18) on a process flow chart. Ask why after each step. If you don't find a logical reason, eliminate the step. Add up the steps (government secretaries in particular should follow this route), put the time saved into dollars, and I'll bet you've saved thousands of dollars in a year's time. The large circle represents operation (anything you do); the small circle, transportation (even if it's from one desk to another); the triangle, storage (even in a box); and the square, inspection (the only non-productive step). The secretary who did the chart shown in Figure 18 figured the process could take two days instead of the present ten days by eliminating steps 7 through 12.

The work count is an analysis of the first two steps. First you followed the people and charted them. Then you followed the process and charted that. Now you take a count and analyze them both to see how many steps can be eliminated. Eliminating steps saves time and *money.*

Finally, a few principles of motion economy may help you save time:

1. The two hands should begin as well as complete their motions at the seme instant. (Haven't you always heard that two hands are better than one?)

Figure 15. Work distribution chart.

Accounting Department—Section 2-A   **Period Ending** ______________

Activities	C.B.A.	Hrs.	I.O.B.	Hrs.	S.B.W.	Hrs.	A.M.H.	Hrs.	L.L.B.	Hrs.
Meetings	Plan				Set up		Attend		Take minutes	
Correspon-dence			Sort		Distribute; answer				File	
Invoices					Approve and sign orders		Approve local purchase invoices		Correspon-dence	
Expense Reports	Approve				Check figures		Get signatures		Type	

Figure 16.   Blank process chart to be filled in.

JOB	SUMMARY		
SUBJECT CHARTED	METHOD	PRESENT	PROPOSED	SAVING
DEPARTMENT	NO. OF OPERATIONS			
SECTION	NO. OF TRANSPORATIONS			
CHARTED	NO. OF STORAGE			
DATE	TIME IN			
	DISTANCE IN FEET			

DIST., FT.	TIME IN	OPER.	TRANS.	STOR.	INSPECT.	STEP NO.	PROPOSED METHOD STEPS IN PROCESS	WHAT? WHO?	WHERE? WHEN?	HOW? WHY?
		◯	○	▽	☐					
		◯	○	▽	☐					
		◯	○	▽	☐					
		◯	○	▽	☐					
		◯	○	▽	☐					
		◯	○	▽	☐					
		◯	○	▽	☐					
		◯	○	▽	☐					
		◯	○	▽	☐					
		◯	○	▽	☐					
		◯	○	▽	☐					
		◯	○	▽	☐					
		◯	○	▽	☐					
		◯	○	▽	☐					
		◯	○	▽	☐					
		◯	○	▽	☐					
		◯	○	▽	☐					
		◯	○	▽	☐					
		◯	○	▽	☐					
		◯	○	▽	☐					

Figure 17. Process chart.

JOB	Processing Expense Accounts for Payment	SUMMARY		
SUBJECT CHARTED	Expense Account Form	METHOD	PRESENT	PROPOSED	SAVING
DEPARTMENT	Accounting	NO. OF OPERATIONS	11	8	3
SECTION	3-B	NO. OF TRANSPORATIONS	8	6	2
CHARTED	X.Y.Z.	NO. OF STORAGE	8	6	2
DATE	7-10	TIME IN	7	4	3
		DISTANCE IN FEET	62	54	8

DIST., FT.	TIME IN	OPER.	TRANS.	STOR.	INSPECT.	STEP NO.	PROPOSED METHOD STEPS IN PROCESS	WHAT? WHO?	WHERE? WHEN?	HOW? WHY?
						1	Receiving Desk (in basket)			
20						2&3	To Distribution Desk (in basket)			
						4	Checked for propriety			
						5	Coded for distribution (applied to voucher jacket)			
						6	Attached to voucher jacket			
4						7&8	To Comptometer Desk (in basket)			
						9	Verified for computation and distribution			
4						10&11	To Posting Machine Operator (in basket)			
						12	Posted to vouchers payable card, distribution			
							sheet, and voucher jacket			
						13	Typewritten to voucher jacket (name & address)			
						14	Attached to voucher copy of voucher jacket			
						15	Listed on transmittal by Elliott-Fisher			
							machine (voucher No. and amount)			
4						16&17	To Distribution Desk (in basket)			
						18&19	Inspected and signed			
12						20&21	To Approval Desk (in basket)			
						22&23	Inspected and signed			
10						24	To outgoing basket			

Figure 18. Process chart.

JOB								SUMMARY			
SUBJECT CHARTED		Correspondence						METHOD	PRESENT	PROPOSED	SAVING
DEPARTMENT		Justice Dept.						NO. OF OPERATIONS			
SECTION		4F						NO. OF TRANSPORATIONS			
CHARTED		O.H.W.						NO. OF STORAGE			
DATE		2/5/79						TIME IN			
								DISTANCE IN FEET			

DIST., FT.	TIME IN	OPER.	TRANS.	STOR.	INSPECT.	STEP NO.	PROPOSED METHOD STEPS IN PROCESS	WHAT? WHO? WHERE? WHEN? HOW? WHY?
						1	Record desk	Record desk
						2	Distribution—Div. Dir.	Directly to branch
						3	Distribution—Branch Chief—Sec.	
						4	Dist.—Area Desk Chief—Sec.	
						5	Dist.—Analyst	
						6	Process corres. answered	
						7	Unit Branch Chief	
						8	Unit Div. Dir.	
						9	Unit Dep. Com.	
						10	Unit Controller	
						11	Unit Corres. Control	
						12	Unit Spec Assist.	
						13	Adm. signs	
						14	Control corres. mailed	
						15	File copy mail back to record desk	
						16	File copy sent to area desk to be filed	

2. The two hands should not be idle at the same instant except during rest periods. (On the other hand, we were always taught to rest one hand in the lap while eating.)

3. Motions of the arms should be made in opposite and symmetrical directions instead of in the same direction and should be made simultaneously. (It may take some time to figure out.)

4. Materials should be located so as to permit the best sequence of motions. (First things first.)

5. Finger and lower arm movements are preferred to upper arm and shoulder movements for light work. (Shoulder to the wheel is not always the best motto.)

6. Rhythm is essential to smooth, automatic performance. (Good for dancing, also.)

7. Materials should be located around the workplace and close to the worker. (Are you always looking for tape, scissors, stickers, and other supplies?)

8. Containers should be used to deliver materials. (Avoid playing pick-up-sticks with deliveries.)

9. "Drop deliveries" should be used wherever possible.

10. The hands should be relieved of all work that can be performed more advantageously by the feet or other parts of the body. (Use discretion!)

11. Continuous curved motions are preferable to straight-line motions involving sudden and sharp changes in directon. (See Principle 3.)

Again, time is never really saved; it's only used wisely or unwisely. As a sage once said, "No man (or woman) is wise at all hours." Nor should be.

5

Communications

"If we could only communicate, . . ." we declare repeatedly in one way or another. Just what does it mean, anyway, when we say we've had a communications failure or breakdown? What exactly are we talking about? And how do we go about communicating?

"When you say something, make sure you have said it," William Strunk, Jr., and E. B. White warn in *The Elements of Style,* because the odds are great that you haven't. Much of this results from not asking yourself: "What is the purpose of this communication? Why am I writing this letter or memo, making this phone call or speech?" Asking yourself why should lead to greater clarity of expression.

In this chapter we'll concentrate on your communications with your boss, clients/customers, co-workers, and subordinates. Questions of communication across age, sex and race will be raised and some suggestions will be offered. We'll touch on how you communicate with the world nonverbally by the clothes you wear and the body language you use. And although we believe the message *is* important, the vehicle with which it's often transmitted—your voice—also carries great weight.

Many secretaries inform us that their biggest problems involve working as a team with their bosses. So let's first structure a method of operations on the premise that a boss and secretary form a team (even if a secretary has more than one boss). Begin now to:

1. Meet at least once a day, even if only for a few minutes, to establish the day's priorities.
2. Always know where to reach a boss who travels. Have full instructions on how to operate in his absence and whom to see in emergencies.
3. Learn precisely what your boss's job requires by asking questions, reading correspondence, learning the significance of the records you keep, and reading in-house publications, bulletin boards, and so forth.
4. Keep the lines of communication open. It may be somewhat circular in a chapter on communications to tell you to "communicate," but if the first three suggestions are followed, you're on the way to fulfilling the last.

Go back the the first step. You and your boss meet to establish the day's priorities. How are you, the secretary, going to make the most of the more-than-likely too few minutes you'll get? Prepare an agenda. Ask yourself beforehand what you want to communicate to him. What is the purpose of this communication? Keep the agenda sharply focused. Don't try to accomplish too much. Get your thoughts in order before you start talking. To avoid crisis deadlines, ask your boss each morning about his plans for the day so that you might begin preparations.

Although the second suggestion deals with knowing the whereabouts of a traveling boss, some bosses "disappear" during the day and might as well be out of town. If you have that kind of boss, try a sign-out sheet placed where he can't miss it when leaving the office. Inquire about any appointments that might have been made without your knowledge. If he's running late for an appointment, suggest that you call the person. In other words, establish with your boss the idea of the two of you as a team, working cooperatively to get the job done. Working as a team is second nature to some bosses, but others might require day-by-day reinforcement.

The third step asks that you learn the requirements of your boss's job. Do you know what his responsibilities are? What is his job, anyway? What division are you in and who are your boss's bosses? Start by informing yourself, and when you've developed a base of information, begin asking questions. Read all correspondence, even if you must scan for the important points. In your other reading, learn to read introductions, chapter headings, and first and last paragraphs if time is short.

Question veteran co-workers who might know the answers. Ask if you might attend meetings even as a note taker. Read other material relevant to the business world, but stay more generally informed as well: All aspects of society interrelate. Attend seminars, join professional associations. Keep the "big picture" in focus. Learn what happened yesterday in your office and what might happen tomorrow.

A leading magazine for secretaries* printed the following quiz, which we have excerpted here:

React to the following statements to determine if you are an effective team. First, get your boss's reaction:

- My secretary and I meet each day at a regularly scheduled time.
- My secretary is able to take care of many problems for me.
- Do I consider the office *my* office or *our* office and us as a *team*?
- Most deadlines are met by our office.
- My secretary offers many suggestions for day-by-day problem solving and ways to improve our team effectiveness.
- I know that things are being handled effectively when I'm away from the office.
- I'd feel comfortable about my secretary's ability to handle the people we serve even if I were away for three or four months.
- I encourage my secretary's professional development and find methods of payment for this education. I even encourage its being done on company time whenever possible.
- I ask my secretary's advice about organizational problem solving.
- I get positive feedback on my secretary's interaction with people outside our office.

Now for your reactions to the following statements:

- All files and backup material are ready for the executive's daily needs.
- With new projects I ask the executive's assistance in setting priorities.

* *The Secretary*, December–January 1981. Reprinted by permission, copyright 1981, *The Secretary*, official publication of Professional Secretaries International, Kansas City, MO.

- I know the organization's goals.
- I project a professional image in our office.
- I'm willing to take on new responsibilities and have communicated this willingness to my boss.
- My ability to organize and my detail-oriented work habits help my boss.
- I know what my boss's job is and what is expected of him and his superiors.
- By coordinating a daily calendar, making travel arrangements, screening phone calls and visitors, and taking other such actions, I save my boss a great deal of time.
- I keep my professional skills up to the minute.
- We can serve as role models for others in the organization.

With continued emphasis on the two of you as a team, we repeat: Read the mail; read what you type; ask questions; research the business you both work for, the world in general, and the place of your business in that world. Stay curious.

THE NEWCOMER

When you are the old hand and your boss is new, how can you orient him? Again, open up lines of communication. Learn his ways, but also express your preferences on how an office should be run. Make sure he has the organization's policies and procedures manual, knows what and when monthly reports are expected, and has samples to study. Give him a typed list of all regularly scheduled meetings, including times and places, and tell him all you know about how the company operates.

For the new secretary in your department, you might provide an organization chart, explain lunch and coffee break schedules, and make sure she has somebody to lunch with, for the first week at least. For her it has to be like being the new kid at school, a little scary. Point out the whereabouts of the powder room, the copy machines, and so on. Provide her with the secretary's manual if she doesn't have one. Maps of her building, plus any others she may need, and initiation into the mysteries of the phone system and the bulletin board policy are also helpful. And helpful is what you're trying to be.

Your communications with your boss occupy a major portion of your day. After all, that's your job. But unless you work in a two-person office, chances are that you've many co-workers in your own or related departments. After an all-day meeting on "effectiveness," secretaries from a large midwestern company shared suggestions on how to improve communications with colleagues:

- Show appreciation for the other person. Communicate face to face. Avoid gossiping.
- Listen. That's truly a rare skill. Don't make snap judgments. Don't anticipate; just listen. And, we might add, don't hear only what you want to hear.
- Accept criticism (see the section on Assertiveness in Chapter 6).
- Be open to suggestions.
- Establish regular department meetings.
- Volunteer to share the workload.
- Be professional in speech, manner, and dress.
- Think before speaking.
- Welcome newcomers as part of the team.
- Get a clear definition of job responsibilities for every department member.
- Treat others as individuals. Avoid prejudice no matter what form it takes: sex, race, or age.

RACE

Face-to-face communication as individuals would seem to be the prescription for reaching across all barriers, but in our culture it's often difficult to achieve across racial lines.

As black Americans are seen more frequently in offices across the country, resentments seem to have grown among both blacks and whites. White secretaries tell us that they have been passed over in favor of black co-workers in order that some "quota" be met. On the other side, the very qualified black secretary resents any implication that she was promoted solely on the basis of race. None of this implies out-and-out racism, but it does suggest that perceptions of fairness depend greatly on your own vantage point.

Some companies are sponsoring groups devoted to bringing these feelings out in the open. They offer discussion groups or groups that emphasize the history of blacks in this country. For some secretaries we've talked to, they've been a revelation. Anything that enhances our knowledge of each other, that recognizes that, in columnist Sydney J. Harris's words, "what unites us as humans is much greater than what divides us," can only be potentially beneficial.

"I have to walk on water," a black secretary starting to move up told us. Afraid not to be perfect, she watches her every move. Others have expressed the fear of moving up because it would reveal deficiencies in their education, cultural knowledge, or other areas. We've talked with white secretaries who are fearful of gossip if they get along well with black male managers. All of this describes the problem, but there is no simple answer. We fall back on the most difficult of all things to do—and that is to see people as individuals, not symbols. You like some individuals, dislike others, but acknowledge that each is as important to himself as you are to you.

SEX

Many men don't take women seriously on the job. Perhaps we should rephrase that. Men probably take women very seriously on the job and resent the fact. At this point, we should stop and confess that what we're doing here smacks of what we warned you against—prejudice. We could say that men don't take *secretaries* seriously, but we bet they'd take *male* secretaries seriously. And it's not just a secretarial concern. Women managers report resistance, subtle or overt, from their male colleagues.

Men will tell you that a major fear is loss of status, of not being considered as important as they were before they worked with women as equals, both in their own and in the organization's eyes. It frequently cuts across racial lines. Secretaries report that black males are as prone to chauvinism as are whites. And women undervalue themselves and other women. Female managers can be as aggressive with both black and white secretaries as men.

But undoubtedly the biggest result of sexual prejudice is economic loss. Equal pay for equal work is meaningless when women compete with other women for low-paying jobs. The depressing figures at this writing are still that women earn $0.59 for every dollar earned by men. In our society, money plays an important role in whether people define themselves as successes or failures. We're not arguing that that's how it should be. In fact, we don't think a person's worth as a human being is at all contingent on money, but it's hard to sell that to somebody who is persistently devalued in the marketplace.

Money is only one way in which sex discrimination shows itself. No doubt the roots go very deep in almost every culture on earth. Face-to-face communication as individuals rather than groups seems to offer the hope of a working relationship here also. However, having said that, we also acknowledge that it is often necessary to function as a member of a group to effect any social change. Ponder the paradox.

AGE

It's been said that age difference is the new barrier between people—the new segregation. Whether or not that's an exaggeration, a difference in style between the generations is often apparent. Frequently, of course, that's all it is: a matter of style. But if it's getting in your way at work, it could become a communications problem. Secretaries themselves suggest some ways that might help. First, forget age. Whatever your age, you are who you are and who you always were. Chances are great that you respond to qualities, not to age.

At times, however, younger secretaries imply that the "older" ones, because of different training and work styles, have trouble sharing workloads. Believing everything they handle for their bosses is "confidential," protective and often possessive, they are sometimes a source of amusement and exasperation to younger secretaries.

Both age groups need to stay understanding and flexible. The younger secretary encountering this attitude should assert herself tactfully when necessary regardless of the age or title of the other person. The key word is "tactfully." The older secretary could ask herself what new ways she could adopt without sacrificing her principles. Above all, young and old need to communicate with each other as individuals, not as members of an age group. Each can gain from the other.

OTHER DEPARTMENTS

There are co-workers, and then there are those who work in other departments. "Them"—up there on the 12th floor where the carpet begins, or in the penthouse, or the mail room, or anyplace where they don't know what they're talking about, where obviously they don't work as hard as your department does, where all the bottlenecks are, and so on. But still, there they are and your department must—what's that word taken from the worlds of both sociology and sewing?—interface with them. Actually, we're talking communications again, no matter what you call it.

Suggestions: Don't forget the obvious. When calling on another department, introduce yourself and identify your department. Then get to your reason for calling, be it request or problem. Be courteous and considerate: A big part of that is to have all the information you need at hand so you don't keep them waiting.

Suppose you're the sales manager's secretary and you're calling the computer center with a request: "Hello, this is Paula Perfect from the sales office. Mr. Loman needs the sales figures, state by state, for the last year. You have the data but it will require some extra programming. Can you please arrange for this to be done or tell me with whom I need to get in touch and how long it is likely to take?"

If your office is called, remember how you like to be treated and be ready to refer the caller to another source if you can't help. The "It's not my job" line got a laugh only on television. It's helpful to know what other departments do and the names of the department heads if you deal with them. Everyone employed by a company has one ultimate goal: the success of the company. It keeps the paychecks coming. It's often all too true that one department affects great indifference or outright antagonism to another department, sometimes making life miserable for those who must try to work with it. It's axiomatic, but worth repeating: You all work for the same place and your paycheck depends on the success of the entire company.

MAKING A SPEECH

If the barriers of age, race, sex, and "we" against "them" are difficult, think about facing a throng of "thems" of all ages, colors, and sexes united as one audience watching you making a speech. A recent survey revealed that the number one fear of Americans, outranking death or dismemberment, is speaking in public. If you're terrified of making a speech, you're not alone—if that's any comfort.

As with any fear, the first thing to do is to acknowledge it openly. A certain amount of fear, a nonparalyzing amount, gives you that edge that makes for a good performance—and making a speech is a performance. Note what actors do. Project to the exit sign or the back row. Keep a varied pace: loud to soft, slow to fast, intense to light. Speak too slowly and your audience will doze off; too quickly and you transmit nervousness.

A small caution about gesturing: When you're on your feet making a speech, if it feels natural to emphasize a point with an appropriate gesture, do so. But don't put them in your talk beforehand. They'll never look natural. If you've watched recent presidents (before Reagan) you'll see what we mean. However, you might mark your speeches with symbols indicating, *slow, fast, voice up,* or *voice down* to vary the rhythm. Take your time; you are in control. Strange as this advice may sound, keep breathing. Don't hold your breath out of tension. Try for a lower tone. If your voice is already high pitched, fear can pitch it even higher. A tape recorder is a valuable tool in helping you to hear both the content of your speech and the way you sound. Don't be frightened by it. Hardly anybody likes the way he sounds.

All right, you've practiced and now project an impossibly perfect combination of traits: crisp, cool, warm, efficient, friendly, and with undertones of Lauren Bacall. But what are you talking about, anyway? As with letters and memos, content and style must form a unit. You must have something to say, must organize the material and then present it in such a way that it interests and informs your audience. Does that sound like a tall order? Maybe, but not out of reach. Remember one essential thing: A speech is an auditory experience, an experience of the ears first and foremost. Don't try to tell everything you know; stick to a few well-focused points. To quote an old formula, "Tell them what you're going to tell them, tell them, and then tell them what you've told them." A speech is not a letter that can be reread to pick up lost points.

Other hints: Index cards are useful in organizing your material. Some people like to jot down important points on these cards and refer to them during their talk. They also give you something to hold to keep your hands still. Luciano Pavorotti, the famous tenor, always carries a handkerchief—as a way of steadying his hands, he says. Before you begin speaking, you can also steady yourself by taking a couple of slow, deep breaths to help allay anxiety. Don't be afraid to pause in your speech; your audience won't get up and go away if you do. But for added insurance against losing the audience, set a time limit.

Remember that a speech is a message for the ears. Make a few points, reiterate them, summarize them, and adhere to your time limit. And smile once in a while. It'll be over soon.

Your voice is the vehicle for your verbal messages. The best speech in the world can be ruined by a screechy, high-pitched voice or a soft, whispery, little-girl tone that you have to strain to hear. Everyday communications that are studded with verbal tics, such as "you know" and "I mean" or the combination play of "you know what I mean?" can put off the listener. If you project sullenness, boredom, a kind of "I couldn't care less" attitude, what can you change (in addition to your attitude, of course)? Your voice, first. Difficult, but not impossible. A tape recorder can be an invaluable but painful tool. Ask yourself these questions objectively: Do I drone on and on in a monotone? Do I sound like fingernails on a blackboard? Do I sound like a little girl? Do I talk too fast to be understood or too slowly to be interesting? Do I sound bored?

If you're really serious about changing a voice you find displeasing, vocal exercise books and speech lessons are available. Groups exist that are devoted solely to public speaking. Two things can be done as a simple beginning: (1) Lower your voice. (2) Eliminate the tics we mentioned. Voices often go high when a person is under tension. When you feel anxious, try breathing evenly and deeply, exhaling slowly for a count of five. For the chronic "you know," some method of behavior modification might work—your own system of rewards and fines or work with a similarly afflicted friend. Again, use the tape recorder.

DRESS

How do you look as you make that speech, chair that meeting, or sit at your desk? Like a secretary? In some circles interested in your "success," that means you've dressed for failure. But take heart, one fashion oracle proclaims that most men and women dress for failure. Neither success nor failure is defined that clearly, but a corporate executive seems to be the model for success and, by implication, a secretary the model for failure—along with all the other people in the world who are not corporate executives.

That kind of definition is insulting to almost everybody, terribly misleading, and often downright silly. Unless you (man or woman) dress the way the oracle dictates, it's virtually impossible for you to succeed. If your clothes don't do it, wear glasses (whether or not you need them) for a "more authoritative look."

Phrases such as "dress for success" have become at least a temporary part of the culture, along with the possibly mythical creatures like the Wall Street lawyer (female) purported to own five interchangeable black suits, or those among us who have more fun— blondes with long hair—being solemnly informed that fun's one thing but you want short dark hair for business. Then there are secretaries like April who wear their strong (slightly masculine-looking) suits and still miss success or even a chance to open their mouths at meetings.

The question is, can you dress for success? We'll give you a definite maybe. No, if it's just window dressing and you lack the foundations of competence, know-how, talent, brains, and industry. Yes, if you've got all that and need a little edge. But beyond the effectiveness of dress as a prerequisite for success, there's the simple question of appropriateness. No doubt competency is often clad in blue jeans; know-how lurks behind too much makeup; talent teeters on too-high heels; brains can wear bangles and bows. Mental lightweights sport Brooks Brothers suits; frauds can be found in gray flannel or the female equivalent. But dress *is* a code, a method of tribal recognition and identification. When you dwell in the land of the conservatively cut three-piece business suit, adhere to the tribal customs if you wish to be taken seriously. If it's not important to you, that's your choice; it's your work that should matter, after all.

Clothes that are "confidently feminine," in the words of

Marianne Talafuse, Purdue University management professor, but not frilly or fussy; makeup that's subdued; jewelry that doesn't distract; heels that let you move without teetering, can add to your chances for increased job responsibilities. We think that a suit (skirt, jacket, and blouse) or a tailored dress, if you prefer, worn with pumps, presents the most businesslike appearance. Look around you and determine what's appropriate where you work. You might work for a disco, where conservative clothes are viewed with suspicion. It's tribal, remember, and as with birds, like flocks with like.

Whatever your "tribe," clothes are high on the list of what people notice about you. Dr. Ashley Montagu recently reported that a survey he conducted shows that people observe (1) physique (bodily appearance), (2) clothes, (3) face, (4) hair, (5) hands. And that brings us to body language.

BODY LANGUAGE

In the same paperback rack with the "dress" books are those on body language. It's enough to make you want to lock yourself up at home. Here you are with your new, well-modulated voice, your authoritative glasses, and your business suit, looking for new worlds to conquer, and you're done in by the set of your shoulders. You've revealed unconscious desires by the crook of your finger. Is it one more thing to worry about? No. Reading body language is only common sense. People have grasped its meaning intuitively since the first caveman slumped before the fire and his wife asked, "What's the matter?" (They spoke English, of course.)

We'd only say that slouching around with a hangdog expression conveys the impression you'd guess it would. Since sometimes *acting* the way you want to feel often produces the feeling, try for good posture and a springy step and see what happens. Things like folded arms give you a closed-off look and seems to be more of a female gesture. Males, in general, use more hand gestures. In some cultures these gestures have quite a colorful repertory of meanings.

Watch that you don't talk with your hand over your mouth. Most people like you to look at them when they're talking to you, but in some groups that's considered arrogant. Indeed, you can make people nervous by staring at them. But if you are open and confi-

dent in your dealings with people, you don't have too much to
worry about.

It's a big subject, communications, covering all the ways we use
language, spoken and written, and all the subtleties of our relationships. It also involves listening well, knowing what questions to ask,
and making sure we've been understood or that we understand
what's been said to or asked of us. Being objective and being
specific are communication skills. And sometimes when you ask
you do receive.

A secretary from a southwestern advertising agency sent us information on the newly organized monthly meetings of the company's senior secretaries. Starting first as an outlet for secretarial
concerns, it plans to develop a problem-solving group. The first
meeting culminated in a written description of the specific responsibilities of the senior secretary, including those that could be delegated. Grievances aired included the need to hire personnel to help
with a work overload in some departments, notably in travel arrangements and equipment purchase, to ease the backup in what
they refer to as "the world of the copy machine." Problems may not
be solved overnight, but thanks to the secretaries who pushed for
the department meetings, a start has been made.

At a large midwestern firm with diversified nationwide interests,
two secretaries communicated their ideas about a development
program for women inside the organization. They took it to the
chairman of the board, and the result was a fully funded, professionally organized program open (by application) to any woman in
the company. Under the direction of two professors from a local
university, the program cited an applicant's "strong desire to enhance (her) individual development" as one criterion for selection.

Although the program will be tailored to the individual participant's needs, certain basic areas are scheduled for the pilot programs, including, of course, communications—verbal skills, listening, and how to say what you mean to say. Under written skills, the
program aimed for the development of a "clear, concise writing
style, and how to write memos and reports." Other areas of communications planned for the program are for using audiovisuals
and planning formal presentations.

We give these examples in some detail, not because the ideas are
new to business, but because they came about in these cases
through the effective use of communications tools by secretaries.

6

Interpersonal Skills

Everything we've discussed could go under the heading of Interpersonal Skills. After all, when we're not dealing with machines, we're dealing with people, on the phone or from behind a desk. Some of them are angry, upset, demanding, or insulting. Others are cooperative and caring. We deal with peers and subordinates, bosses and board chairman, and we try to understand them as well as ourselves.

In this chapter the intangibles of loyalty and confidentiality will be considered, and we will take a more extensive look at day-to-day dealings on the job. We spoke about being open and confident earlier. In the Assertiveness section you'll learn a method of increasing your confidence in yourself and a style of openness that is not hurtful to others. But first let's talk about loyalty.

LOYALTY

Loyalty is much prized in dogs and soldiers, political cronies, and sports fans. It's abused when it's subverted to the blind support of leaders in the wrong. How about the loyalty of secretaries? For super-secretaries like Rosemary Wood—remember Watergate?—it became a way of life. Where do your loyalties lie, anyway—with your boss or with the company? In Wood's case, the "company" was her country, but that apparently was an abstraction to her compared with a flesh-and-blood boss.

It's a human dilemma, we grant. But here's a small test of that principle for you: You are a confidential secretary working for a vice-president. Another vice-president walks into your boss's office (she is not there) and starts going through the unlocked drawers. What do you do? Start by asking: "May I help you find something?" If the answer is "No, I can find it," assert yourself and say: "Mrs. Smith does not want anyone to look through her desk."

Now how about the same scenario with the chairman of the board or the president of the company as the "intruder"? What do you do? Nothing. You and your boss are both professionals who work for the company; you are not employed by your boss. If you are then asked to keep the visit confidential, you should do just that. But being human, assert yourself and say, "I feel uncomfortable about doing that."

Many secretaries have told us that they *would* inform their bosses about their superiors' actions. If you are one of them, tell the chairman and/or president "I can't promise I'll do that," and take your chances. We don't pretend that either is the ideal solution. Of course you feel loyal to your boss if you have a good working relationship with him or her, but you should think out what that means and where higher loyalties are involved. On the subject of loyalty, don't forget loyalty to yourself, which is what the following section is all about.

ASSERTIVENESS

Remember "Sherry, get in here, I need you," hollered by the boss from an inner office when Sherry is on the phone with a call or busy in any number of ways? Sherry doesn't like it—neither the tone, nor the "hollering," nor the imperiousness of it. What should she do?

The seminar group considered the possible solutions. How could she convey to her boss that she didn't like it? Had she, as a matter of fact, told him she didn't like the hollering? She had, she said, but he still yelled.

From across the room a voice called out, "I'd tell him to stick it." Everybody laughed, including Sherry. Assertive, no; aggressive, yes. It would be briefly satisfying; but, of course, no real solution unless you were on the way out the door to another job.

"I'd tell him to stick it." It's one solution. How about ignoring the summons? Crying? Pleading? What should Sherry do?

How about Janet lying for her boss, or Bonnie and the cheating lawyer? When visitors or co-workers drop by for a chat, do you inform them that you're busy at the moment? Can you get the reports your boss wants from other managers without getting the runaround? Can you refuse a contribution to yet another office collection or handle an aggressive salesman in person or on the phone? Think of examples from your own office. How do you deal with authority or cope with the feelings of intimidation that many secretaries report having?

"So many things work toward giving you that intimidated feeling," Bonnie said. "You're always aware that they (the bosses) have the power and you don't and they have many subtle ways of keeping it that way."

If you've read *When I Say No, I Feel Guilty* by Manuel (Pete) Smith, Ph.D., you should have a good idea of how to deal with those feelings. One of the founders of assertiveness training, Dr. Smith started using the method on the West Coast in veterans' hospitals as a way of dealing with patients' emotional problems. Unfortunately, many who picked it up later confused aggressiveness with assertiveness. Assertiveness is the opposite of aggressiveness; a nonassertive person can frequently be quite aggressive.

For use in social conflict situations, assertive behavior doesn't aim at "winning" or helping you get your own way. It seeks solely to save or improve your self-esteem. Any other result is a by-product. If you're nonassertive, you don't stand up for your rights, seldom express or even acknowledge your feelings or thoughts, and often end up depressed, nervous, anxious, or possibly ill. On the other hand, if you're aggressive, you do express all those things and probably quite often; but, in doing so, you frequently step on the rights of others, making you feel guilty, and rightly so.

Assertive behavior holds you responsible for your own words and actions. It teaches you how to express yourself without putting anybody else down; it doesn't play the seesaw game of intimidation. As Joyce Dudney Fleming, Ph.D., expresses it, "With intimidation on your side, no one else will be."

Neither a "fight" (aggressive) nor a "flight" (nonassertive) reaction, assertiveness puts you in control of yourself.

But it's not as easy as it sounds.

First, we'll start with a few communications principles. When speaking to your boss, we recommend using the pronoun "we"; for example, "We have a problem." When talking to a peer or subordinate, "you" is preferable: "What do you think?" If you feel a conflict arising—you're getting that old queasy feeling in your stomach—that's the time for assertion and the pronoun "I." (Even if you are the only one to perceive the situation as a conflict, it's time to assert. You have a right to your feelings.)

Unfortunately, most people act in the reverse way. They communicate in a series of "I's": "I want it done this way" or "Let me tell you about my trip, my party, my new dress." In conflict, they resort to "you." "You shouldn't have done that." "You always do that." "You never do what you're supposed to." Can you see the difference among these ways of expressing yourself?

Of course, we're all nonassertive, assertive, or aggressive with different people in different situations. We're not always intelligent about our self-expression. But the more (truly) assertive we become, the better we feel about ourselves and others. Everybody benefits. If a boss (or anyone) puts us down and we don't assert ourselves, allowing the annoyance to grow into anger and taking it out on innocent co-workers or friends, the snowball starts rolling: The chairman picks on your boss, your boss snaps at you, you insult a co-worker, and pity the dog when she gets home.

On the average, 20 out of 25 secretaries attending our seminars have told us they would rather work for a man than a woman. In part we think it's because women, through inexperience with positions of authority, sometimes confuse aggressiveness with assertiveness. It's often the same with male middle managers who don't think they'll ever advance. As a general rule, people at the top are assertive. Self-confident and powerful, they delegate responsibilities to people under them without fearing a subordinate's mistakes. At this writing, as more opportunities open up for women to advance, fewer secretaries care if their boss is male or female.

Not surprisingly, most secretaries believe themselves to be nonassertive. After an afternoon of assertiveness training at a recent seminar, one woman told the group that while she had always considered herself assertive, she'd have to say she'd really been aggressive. But others have allowed themselves to be needlessly intimidated and sometimes verbally abused. We think everyone needs assertiveness training (bosses as well, but that's not our concern here). Learning assertive responses is like learning a different language. It takes a while before you can "think" in it. We'll go over the responses first, then give you some examples.

The first and easiest to learn is the simple *repeating* method, used only with strangers.

The second response involves *expressing yourself,* using the pronoun "I." What is it *I* want, don't want, feel, like, or don't like?

The third is acknowledgment or *agreement,* if you will. More later on this difficult response.

The dialogs in this chapter describe work situations, but the technique also works well in your personal life. One area of your life affects another, after all.

How does repeating work? Try this technique as an ice-breaker, a way of easing into assertiveness. The doorbell rings. It's a salesman (and remember, he's just doing his job).

"Good morning, ma'am. How are you today? Good, good. Do you like housework? No, of course you don't. Well, I have here the Little Handy Homemaker, guaranteed to do everything but cook dinner. If I can have a minute of your time and show you. . . ."

You are *not* interested. What do you say? Do you mumble something about your husband not being there right now?

"I'll be back later," he answers.

"I'm busy," you try again.

"I'll come back anytime you wish," he offers.

"I already have a vacuum cleaner," you lie shamelessly.

"Not like this one. . . . If I could just demonstrate it," he persists.

Enough! You get the idea. It's the salesman's job to take advantage of any opening you give him. If you're not interested, *say so,* and say so repeatedly. No matter what he says, you say, "I'm not interested." If he persists longer than you think necessary, repeat that you're not interested and say you're going to close the door now. Remember, this is a person you don't know. The technique saves both of you time. Simple? Yes.

Now suppose you do know the person. It's not a friend but, say, a neighbor from down the street or a worker from another department who is collecting for something to which you do not wish to contribute. Your reasons are your own. You can say politely, "I'm not interested." If she persists or asks for explanations, remember that you don't owe one; you have no need to justify yourself. If she insists, tell her how you feel or what you want. Express yourself. You might tell her, "I don't want to continue this conversation. It's making me uncomfortable." Generally speaking, the other person has no choice but to wind down.

So far, so good. Now it gets a little more difficult. It's your boss or co-worker (on the home front, it's your husband, child, mother) and the stakes are higher. Maybe, as several secretaries reported to us, your heart pounds a little bit at first, but you're not in a contest of wills. Your boss, for example, has more *power* than you but you are *equal* as human beings. You're not interested in diminishing him; neither are you willing to be diminished by him.

So what about Janet and Bonnie and their bosses, who have involved them in lying and cheating? Have you figured out what Sherry should do? Of course. She should tell her boss, "I don't like to be yelled at." She should express herself. Notice that she does not tell him what to do; she simply reports her likes and dislikes about how she is being treated. A simple one-liner, but a secretary at a recent seminar reported telling her boss something similiar— he was a yeller also—and a great intake of breath went through the room.

Janet and Bonnie could also use one-liners. Janet, for instance, could say, "I like working for you but I'm not comfortable lying for you." Bonnie did take assertive action in her letter to the lawyer about his fraudulent record keeping. It was effective, at least for the time she was employed by him. In no case does anybody tell anybody else what to do. Each person is expressing her own feelings or wishes.

Maybe Sherry's boss will continue to yell. She can't change him; she can only react to his behavior. Maybe Sherry will continue to tell him how she feels about it. Maybe she'll decide to go elsewhere to work, or maybe he'll stop yelling. The outcome is secondary to expressing yourself when you are truly bothered by someone else's actions.

More than one secretary has been bothered by the Coffee Question, symbolic of personal work in general. Some object and some don't. What if you do? Most secretaries tell us they don't mind favors done on a person-to-person basis, but resent serving coffee as a job requirement. (Parenthetically, we might note that a recent 600-person survey by a 3M unit and the National Secretaries Association found that only 53 percent of those surveyed serve coffee or food, the aspect of secretarial work identified as least satisfying.)

How about you? It's a difficult question to discuss without sounding petty. So make up your own mind, with some guidelines to help: If, as one secretary we know says, serving coffee to a room full of people after it's delivered by the company's cafeteria not only takes her time but makes her feel uncomfortably like a tearoom hostess, what should she do? She's told her boss she doesn't mind ordering the coffee but would prefer not to serve it. He feels just as strongly about her doing it. (He likes the idea, she said, of her acting like a gracious hostess.) Impasse. Well, we suggest she continue but request a job description from him that will delineate her duties. It's an assertive action and allows room for compromise.

If you feel no compromise is possible on this issue, be prepared. A recent news item in the *Chicago Sun-Times* reported the case of a clerk-typist (not secretary) who told her boss, when ordered to go out and get him coffee, to get it himself. For that, she was suspended for one day, and recently an arbitrator upheld the suspension. Even if getting coffee wasn't part of her job description, the arbitrator said, the rule is "obey now and grieve later."

We agree, plus "get it yourself," if it's a literal quote, is telling another person what to do. Grieve later, by all means, if you wish. Express your feelings: "I'll get the coffee now, but I really don't believe it's part of my job and I would like a job description outlining my duties."

Asking for a job description and writing a letter outlining your thoughts about pay fraud, as Bonnie did, are both assertive actions expressing what you think and feel about a situation affecting you. Another common work situation involves a different type of assertive action. Many secretaries, charged with getting reports from other managers for their bosses, have the responsibility for seeing that the reports are handed in on time, but they have no authority over the other managers. Frequently, they are put off by other secretaries who, after trying unsuccessfully to collect overdue work from one manager, was told by him the next time she asked, "I'm sorry I recommended you for your job. If you don't leave me alone, I'm going to derecommend you." She asked him what she should do about future follow-up items. "Ignore them," he said.

Secretaries have tried memos, predating, nagging. Most resist going back to their bosses and reporting failure. We feel that a secretary who is given the responsibility for collecting reports should have the authority to go directly to the manager. If she gets no response, she should inform her boss, and then write "no response" after the manager's name when she submits the material. Of course, we're not taking a rigid hard line; people have the right to know when you're changing your policy; busy people often need reminders. But when, in your judgment, the situation warrants it, do it. You're no longer going to "bother" or "nag." Your time is important, too. It's a form of assertive action.

Let's go back to the vice-president's secretary and her conversation with the manager, who, incidentally, was her former boss. He tells her he's "sorry he recommended her for the job. If you don't leave me alone, I'm going to derecommend you." How should she handle that remark? Both professionally and assertively, we believe it's better if she ignores it and presses on with her business: getting the report or the follow-up items from him. "Mr. Jones needs that report from you by 4 o'clock this afternoon," she could say in response. As for asking him what she should do with future requests for follow-up items, we think it would have been better not to have asked him in the first place. It's her job to get the reports and to do the follow-ups. She hasn't got the option of ignoring them.

The problem of responsibility without authority—some believe it is the biggest factor in causing stress—is faced by secretaries every day. What are the lines of authority? Can you keep unannounced visitors from your boss if he has asked you to? Will he uphold you if you do? Has he given you the "cloak of authority" to wear? A few secretaries report that they sometimes get the blame for doing things they've been told to do when it's convenient to shift the responsibility to them. Assertiveness, whether in words or actions, may not solve all these problems, but it will bring them out in the open and at least enhance the possibility of a solution. And, of course, your self-esteem as a *professional* dealing with other professionals will increase.

As a professional secretary, you may frequently find yourself dealing with subordinates. Assertiveness can carry you through conflict situations when you might be uncomfortable with your authority.

"I have to deal with a clerk-typist," Lois Starr told us, "who is an 'arguer' about any work she is given to do. Finally, one day when I felt totally frustrated by her, I told her to shape up or ship out, and I'm afraid I was yelling. Well, I was so upset by the encounter that I cried in the ladies' room. The clerk-typist got more sullen and nothing was settled."

We're not going to attempt any amateur psychology here, but we will just say that if you play an arguer's game you are acting at his level and are bound to lose (you are being controlled) or at least lose your temper. Lois is the authority here. By arguing, she is letting the clerk-typist know she doesn't believe in her own power. Instead, give the work to the typist, tell her what is expected of her and when—maybe even agree that the work is hard—but take for granted that it will be done. "I expect it by tomorrow morning."

Jennifer has a situation with a copy boy who refuses to do work for her that she believes to be part of his job. It's becoming an ongoing problem.

"I'll have to go to your supervisor," she told him after another refusal. This was a proper assertive action. She didn't get into an argument. Trying to solve the problem by getting a statement about the copy boy's job requirements is another assertive action response. Is it his job or isn't it? She (and he) needs to know so they both can perform their duties. Again, it's important for people to have clear ideas of what their jobs require.

One thing your job does not require is any sexual favors. More and more women are fighting (and winning) the issue in court, backed now by Title VII of the Civil Rights Act of 1964. In a landmark 1977 decision, a U.S. Court of Appeals for the District of Columbia Circuit ruled that hiring a woman for a job with sexual strings attached violates the law under Title VII. (In this case Paulette Davis was appealing the decision after losing her first complaint against the abolition of her job with the office of Equal Employment Opportunity, because, her claim stated, she refused to have an "affair" with her employer.) We're going to assume it's not going to reach that point with you, that you won't let it start, however innocent it may seem at first.

Secretaries have told us that it is crucial to "be professional." And by all means, Cara Thompson emphasized: "Keep your mouth shut (about sexual comments made to you) around co-workers. Don't be an object of gossip." If all else fails, keep a detailed log. Ask for an appointment with your EEO officer and give dates, times, and places and describe the situation and what was said, especially if any promises or threats were made. Ask that your statement be put in your personnel file and write it yourself. (There's more on sexual harassment in Chapter 10.) The point is, you're not a passive victim. You can initiate assertive action when it's appropriate.

In expressing yourself in a work situation, using verbs such as "want," "like," and "don't like" is preferable to expressions of feelings. Save those for personal encounters. Each person will have a different assertive "I" message or method of expression but the structure should be the same. Defensive statements or explanations are inclined to lower your self-esteem; by implication, they give the other person more rights than you have. The other person can simply make a statement, but you have to explain your position. Paraphrasing St. Augustine: "Do what you want but don't hurt anyone."

A friend of ours, catching onto the expressing technique, now claims she knows better than to say, "You, sir or madam, are an idiot." Instead, she now says: "I feel, sir or madam, that you are an idiot." Good try, but not quite. Try: "I am annoyed" or "I am angry."

Now, at last, we come to our favorite response, which is also the most difficult: *agreeing* or acknowledging. (Remember, all these responses can be used singly or in combination. Usually one-liners, they can save you many sleepless nights regretting what you either said or didn't say. Spend your energy on the constructive things in life.)

But back to *agreeing* or acknowledging: What you're agreeing with is criticism. Imagine that you're at your desk at work, typing, on the phone with a client, or adding up figures, and a colleague walks by and tells you angrily, "Get down from the bookcase; you certainly look silly perched up there." Raving mad, you'd think;

that person has gone round the bend. Would you be upset or hurt by his statement, or even resent being called silly? You'd be puzzled, perhaps; but not wounded. If, however, that same person said to you, "You're really stupid" or "You are the most inconsiderate person I've ever met," your reaction would no doubt be quite different.

Why? What's the difference? Well, it's obvious that there's no truth to the first statement. It's nonthreatening. But, the second comment many contain an *element* of truth. Only an element? Nonassertive people feel they have to be perfect in order to like themselves. Letting everyone judge them, they wait for every verdict; when it's negative they fight against it, but they believe it.

Columnist Sydney J. Harris describes the "perpetual reactor," swinging from euphoria when praised to depression when criticized. There seems to be no stable center, no equanimity in the personality. On the other hand, while acknowledging weakness and behavior patterns they would like to change, assertive people respect themselves and others. So be your own judge: You know how lazy you are, how selfish, and maybe how stupid. One of Manuel Smith's students once said to him, "How can you agree when I call you stupid?" "Because," Smith answered, "compared with Einstein I am dumb. I do dumb things every day." Don't we all? The *element* of truth is what he's agreeing with.

"Nothing human is foreign to me"—those old Greeks again. Being assertive doesn't mean being manipulative or indulging in game playing that lowers self-esteem. It does mean being honest. For example, you're told that you are stupid. If you're a Smith you could say, "You're right. At times I'm a real dumb-dumb." If you're just halfway there and such comments hurt or anger you or threaten you in any way, you could say, "You're right, but I don't like to be criticized." In personal situations, you might say, "You're right, but your saying so hurts my feelings."

So when boss, husband, or friends criticize you (and they are dealing in reality; they don't see you swinging from the chandelier), look for the element of truth in what they say. Agree with that element matter-of-factly. Assess whether or not it's something you'd like to change, but don't take it as an indictment of your whole character and personality. Accept *all* of yourself and your self-esteem will go up ten notches. Simple? No.

Smith drew up a little list of assertive rights we all have: the right not to care, the right not to be logical (our favorite with lawyers), the right not to understand, the right not to know, and *the right to make mistakes*. Recent history is replete with the disastrous cover-ups of presidents and corporations: Openness in admitting mistakes would have been far less costly to us all.

So *repeat, express,* and *agree.*

To remove this discussion from abstraction to reality, we are including some assertive dialogs based on situations secretaries have reported to us:

SECRETARY AND SECRETARY—PERSONALITY

Secretary:	Hi, how are you?
Peer:	(No response.)
Secretary:	(Feels bad; this happens all the time. When they have to work together, she gets no dialog, but lots of dirty looks.) I like to have people answer me.
Peer:	Really?
Secretary:	Yes.
Peer:	(No response.)
Secretary:	I'd like to discuss something with you that's been bothering me.
Peer:	What?
Secretary:	I feel we have a problem communicating.
Peer:	Really?
Secretary:	I'd like to discuss it.
Peer:	I don't think we have anything to discuss.
Secretary:	That may be (agrees).
Peer:	So.
Secretary:	I'd like us to be able to talk without this feeling of hostility.
Peer:	I just don't like you.
Secretary:	That hurts my feelings, but I'd like it not to interfere with our work.

This exchange may seem unlikely, but it was reported almost verbatim to us. The peer was assertive and expressed herself, which is her right. It's better to be blunt than to express feelings indirectly. Hostilities eventually surface. Sometimes being assertive hastens the inevitable. However, the secretary also has the right to self-expression. Although the above exchange will still hurt, the hurt will be lessened by acknowledging that it's okay to be vulnerable; it's less damaging to the ego. As your self-esteem increases, the opinions of others won't be as crucial. It's nice to be liked, but it's essential to like yourself first.

APRIL AND BOSS—PERSONALITY

Then there's April and her boss Susan, who told her to "work on her personality." Assertion includes admitting mistakes and sometimes the wish to change certain less desirable traits. Once you have got your ego in shape, try asking a series of questions:

April:	What traits do you want me to work on?
Susan:	(Unassertively, because she didn't get right to the point.) Your dealings with clients.
April:	With what clients?
Susan:	Mr. Smith and Mrs. Brown.
April:	In what way would you like me to change?

Given an opening, the boss should tell her so she can work on it. Only if you know what you're doing wrong can you change and improve.

SECRETARY AND TYPIST—DELEGATION

Secretary:	Typist, I know you're busy but I'd like you to help me type this report that's due Friday. (Expresses.)
Typist:	That's your job.
Secretary:	That's true, but I need help with it. (Agrees and expresses.)
Typist:	You have more time.
Secretary:	I'd like you to type this by Friday. (Repeats and expresses.)
Typist:	Get someone else to do it.
Secretary:	I'd like you to type this. (Repeats and expresses.)
Typist:	I have too much work to do.

Secretary:	We'll look into your workload, but now I'd like you to type this report. (Agrees and repeats and expresses.)
Typist:	(Sighs.) Geez. . . . (Resentful.)
Secretary:	Thank you. I'll pick it up Friday about 2:00. (Exits.)

Ignore the resentment. You're a professional, paid to do a job, not to win popularity contests. If the typist does have a heavy workload, you can look into it. Even if she's aggressive and passive, she might still have a legitimate beef.

In the next situation, the setting is different. The older woman resents the young secretary who is making as much as she is. A 20-year company veteran, the older woman is protecting her territory. Both report to the same boss. The younger secretary carries a large workload and is constantly asked to do the older one's work. The boss, who knows the situation, won't fire the older secretary. Surly and resentful, the older secretary, however understandably, is causing the younger secretary's work to suffer.

OLDER WOMAN AND SECRETARY

Older Woman:	I feel lousy today. Could you get 30 copies of this report run off by this afternoon?
Secretary:	(From under a pile of paperwork.) No, I can't. (Expresses.)
Older Woman:	Mr. Simons needs these copies today.
Secretary:	I'm sure it's important, but I don't have time. (Agrees and expresses.)
Older Woman:	What are you working on?
Secretary:	I have priority work to do. (Expresses.)
Older Woman:	This has more priority. Mr. Simons said so.
Secretary:	(Tempted to say "Then you do it.") I have priority work to do. (Repeats and expresses.)
Older Woman:	Who said so?
Secretary:	I have this work to do. (Repeats and expresses.)
Older Woman:	I've been here longer and I know this is more important.
Secretary:	Yes, you have been here longer. (Agrees.)

Older Woman:	You think you know it all.
Secretary:	I don't like to be put down. (Express yourself. Don't get aggressive or defensive or explain.)
Older Woman:	Well, how do you think I feel?
Secretary:	I have to get back to work now. (Expresses and repeats.)
Older Woman:	I'll leave this report and you can work on it later.
Secretary:	I am not doing it. (Expresses.)
Older Woman:	You think you're a princess.
Secretary:	I don't care to continue this discussion. (Expresses.)

You might try communicating at a later date when it's not a conflict situation: "I'd like to have lunch with you to discuss something that's been on my mind." Then at lunch you might tell her, "I think we have a problem." Explain that you feel uncomfortable and would like to get along better. Maybe the older secretary just needs someone to understand her feelings.

BOSS AND SECRETARY—OVERTIME

As a professional, you'll be required to work overtime when there's a crisis. If your boss constantly has overtime work, he has a time-management problem. Remember Rebecca and Saturday work?

Boss:	Rebecca, could you come in Saturday afternoon and finish this report?
Secretary:	No, I can't come in the afternoon.
Boss:	Why?
Secretary:	Personal reasons.
Boss:	What's so important?
Secretary:	It's personal.
Boss:	This is urgent.
Secretary:	I will come in Saturday morning early. If that won't do, I can get someone else to do it. (Offer solutions.)
Boss:	It's confidential. Only you can do it and I prefer the afternoon.
Secretary:	I can't on Saturday afternoons.
Boss:	What am I going to do? I need this.

Secretary:	I know you're in a bind. I can't come in, but I can get Mary to do it.

He'll find a solution—or maybe manage his time better.

But there are times when even the best-managed department gets overloaded.

SHARING THE WORKLOAD

Secretary A:	Can you help me with this report? I'm loaded down with work. (Expresses.)
Secretary B:	I can't. I've got too much work of my own to do. (Expresses.)

In this situation both A and B are assertive and there's no conflict. But look at the case of C and D:

Secretary C:	Can you help me with this report?
Secretary D:	(A peer who is filing her nails and glancing through a magazine.) It's not my job. Do it yourself. (Aggressive.)
Secretary C:	You're right. It is my job, but I would appreciate the help. (Agrees and expresses.)
Secretary D:	If you can't manage your workload, I don't see why I should have to help. (Aggressive and nonassertive.)
Secretary C:	This report must be done and I want you to help me. (Repeats and expresses.)
Secretary D:	Get someone else. (Aggressive.)
Secretary C:	I want you to help. (Repeats and expresses.)
Secretary D:	Why me? (Passive/aggressive.)
Secretary C:	I don't have time for explanations. This report must be done. (Expresses.)
Secretary D:	If I have time. (Nonassertive.)
Secretary C:	I need it by 5:00 on Thursday. (Expresses.)
Secretary D:	I said if I have time. Don't bug me. (Aggressive.)
Secretary C:	I'll inform the accounting department that you and I are both working on it. (Expresses.)

(Use your boss's name, but always try to settle differences without going to the boss with personal problems. As a responsible adult, you can handle them.)

It's an unwritten law in some corporations—and it should be in all—that if one department is overworked, other sections in other departments will help out.

Finally, a problem that few women in the workforce have not had to manage:

SEXUAL HARASSMENT

Scene: Secretary bending over filing cabinet.

Male: Wow, I sure like the view from here.

Secretary: I don't like that remark. (Expresses.)

Male: You're awfully touchy.

Secretary: Yes. (Agrees.)

Male: Come on. That's a compliment. You've got a cute little bottom.

Secretary: I am getting annoyed. (Expresses, repeats.)

Male: Come on, you love it. Look at those sexy clothes you wear. You want men to look at you.

(Here's a good place to show different possible responses.)

Secretary: I am getting angry. (Assertive.) (Exits.)

or

I do not! I wear these clothes because they're stylish. (Nonassertive. You don't owe him an explanation.)

or

Go to hell. (Aggressive. You're going to end up in a verbal free-for-all, damaging your self-esteem and controlled by him.)

Sexual harassment is frequently verbal. When the situation disturbs you, use assertiveness. At least 70 percent of working women report having been sexually harassed by males at some time. (See also Chapter 10.) The law now protects women against such harassment and incidents seem to be on the downswing. Threats or promises of job promotions for sexual favors are on the wane (not entirely gone), but sexual innuendo still hangs on. We believe it can be handled assertively. Don't feel resentful if somebody else chooses the primrose path and achieves success. Stick to your job and do it well.

Note: We understand that some women, playing the male game, have been chasing men in the executive suite. Also, some men are intimidated by fear of lawsuits and are overreacting. For example, some keep the door open when dictating. And there's the timid treasurer who asked a secretary we know please to take the new, attractive secretary to the water cooler at four o'clock. His wife was coming and he'd told her all the secretaries were ugly. Well, it does make the world go round, but does it get the work done? Maybe it was the same man who was caught in this situation:

THE JEALOUS WIFE

Scene: Office party.
Cast: Secretary, young and pretty
                          Boss's wife, older (and drunk)
                          Boss

Young secretary, having danced with her boss once, is sitting at the bar when the wife walks up.

Wife: You look like a whore.
Secretary: (In real life she was too shocked to speak. Nonassertive, but we'd all probably react much the same way. But we'll continue in case it ever happens to you.)
                          You old biddy. (Aggressive.)
                          or
                          I want an apology. (Assertive.)

Of course, she wouldn't get the apology, but she could have salvaged her self-image, which is what assertiveness is all about. She could feel good about herself knowing she had the right to express her feelings. In case you think by not speaking the secretary stopped a confrontation, think again.

Scene: One hour later, at the same office party. The secretary is sitting at the bar talking to a friend when the wife walks up and throws a glass of whisky at *her*.

The assertive response might be different for all of us, but the structure would be the same. We might say: "I'll send you the bill." (We like that one.) Other possible responses: "I'm thoroughly disgusted." "I am furious." "I want an apology." But keep in mind it's difficult to assert with drunks. Refrain from any conflict and say "I'll discuss this with you later."

If you get discouraged when you act like a doormat, or lose control and get aggressive, remember that few people are candidates for sainthood. Assertiveness, properly understood, is a process, not a termination point. Nobody ever arrives, but with practice the route does become easier to take.

7
Motivation

GIVING SCOPE TO YOUR LIFE

The ancient Greeks, who believed in developing the body, the spirit, and the mind, defined happiness as "fulfilling all your capacities along the lines of excellence in a life that gives them scope." Modern motivational research into the workforce has been confirming what the ancients knew all along: A happy person is a person who leads the good life by fulfilling all his needs. That's what Aristotle believed. Moderns like Abraham Maslow, Frederick Herzberg, and David McClelland all propound motivational theories that expand on this precept.

What motivates you? What makes you move in a direction that will be to your long-term benefit (and the good of the organization for which you work)?

Motivating workers is a problem for many managers today. In the past, you counted yourself lucky just to have a job. It takes more than that to satisfy today's worker. Many companies, in an effort to improve motivation and, therefore, production, are trying greater worker participation. A General Motors plant in Tarrytown, N.Y., for example, became GM's number one producer after starting a program of worker participation in company decisions. Companies that adopt greater worker participation discover that workers have good ideas on ways to increase production and cut costs. Everybody benefits—company, manager, and worker. The worker ends up with a renewed sense of achievement.

It's no different when secretaries are brought into the decision-making process. They, too, become more highly motivated. Secretaries have told us repeatedly of their need for respect, recognition, and increased job responsibilities, but they also mention salary as a prime mover. How do these separate things work as motivators?

Let's listen to what our experts say about how you are motivated and what your needs are. Maslow's explanation of the hierarchy of needs is probably the best known of all. Starting with the basic physiological needs at the bottom of the scale, Maslow claims people arrange their needs in levels of priority, moving up through safety and security, the social needs for love and belongingness, and the ego needs of esteem and self-respect to self-actualization (growth) needs.

According to Maslow, the needs at the bottom of the scale must be satisfied before a person is motivated at the next level. In other words, if your basic needs for food, water, and shelter aren't met, there's not much use in discussing self-actualization or even security needs. Somebody once said: "People live by bread alone where there is no bread."

Herzberg explains it this way: Satisfied workers are motivated by intrinsic or internal factors—"motivators" such as recognition, responsibility, a sense of achievement, growth, and fulfillment. "Hygienic" factors—extrinsic factors or externals such as salary, status, security, rules, supervision, and relationships—move the dissatisfied worker. Like Maslow's, Herzberg's theory holds that "hygienic" factors are prerequisites for effective motivation but by themselves do not motivate. Requiring constant attention and renewal, maintenance needs in and of themselves don't lead to satisfaction. Job satisfaction develops through the "motivator" of job enrichments that permit greater achievement for the worker.

Herzberg's theory cautions that "hygienics" must be improved before "motivators" are offered. Secretaries justifiably want more salary, but none we know would claim satisfaction with money alone. They seek such intrinsic factors as respect, recognition, more responsibility, and growth possibilities. Because secretaries are "hard to find," they are now (1982) commanding better pay and broader work responsibilities than they have in the past. "There's a phenomenal market out there," an official of the Katherine Gibbs Secretarial Schools claims.

Psychologist David McClelland, measuring the need for achievement in his motivational theory, states that the drive toward constructive activity is the essence of work. He claims that some people have a higher need for achievement than others, achieving through intrinsic/internal factors. That leads us to the famous (or infamous) Theory X and Theory Y views of people at work. In brief, Theory X says people are governed by externals. They need control. Their behavior must be modified to fit the organization's needs. Theory Y people, on the other hand, are internal personality types. They are capable of motivating themselves and don't need to be driven.

In reality, most of us are motivated by a combination of things, are moved by both internal and external factors. Edward Thorndike thought the basic principle of motivation could be defined as "the law of effect," applicable to both animal and human behavior. Rewarding a behavior, Thorndike theorized, *increases* the probability of the behavior's being repeated in the future, while punishing a behavior *decreases* the likelihood that the behavior will be repeated. Rewards stamp in; punishment stamps out.

Julian Rotter took the conditioning principle a step further: People, having greater memory capacities than animals, develop expectations about rewards and punishments. Rotter claimed that people then begin to predict the source of the rewards or the punishments. For example, do you believe in luck, fate, or chance—those old external factors? Theory X people may. Theory Y people tend to believe that their own actions control whether they are punished or rewarded.

Now on to you, the secretary. Keeping in mind that work has financial, social, technical, psychological, and sociological elements, how much job satisfaction do you have? What's important to you? Here's a list of things for you to mark (1) top priority, (2) moderately important, or (3) doesn't really matter. Mark the list according to your first reaction to the statement.

______ Leisure time

______ Time to be with my family

______ Job security

______ Being boss

_____ Recognition by superiors
_____ Recognition by others
_____ Being well liked
_____ A sense of individuality
_____ Constant challenge
_____ No surprises
_____ Being needed
_____ Sense of achievement
_____ Being right
_____ Finishing first
_____ Pleasant surroundings
_____ Working with compatible people
_____ Working alone
_____ Vacation time
_____ Size of company
_____ Having a male boss
_____ Having a married boss
_____ Political work
_____ Not knowing what I'll be doing next year
_____ Travel time to and from work
_____ Location
_____ Leaving work on time
_____ A good salary with the promise of raises
_____ Rules and regulations
_____ Potential of promotion
_____ Direct control of other secretaries
_____ Work that influences others
_____ Creative opportunities
_____ Activities with co-workers after hours
_____ Work that gratifies me
_____ Benefits package

If you checked off more external factors as top priority than internal factors, you're probably not satisfied with your job and are not truly motivated. Conversely, if you marked a greater number of internal factors as top priority, you're a motivated worker, a self-starter. Things such as being well liked, location, and time off are externals, whereas the need for challenge or recognition and a chance to be creative are internal factors.

Of the following, what is the most important to you? Start at 12 and list in descending order:

_______ Money
_______ Status
_______ Rules
_______ Supervision
_______ Power
_______ Recognition
_______ Security
_______ Independence
_______ Duty
_______ Responsibility
_______ Relationships
_______ Sense of fulfillment

Most secretaries, according to our seminar results, give "economic security" top priority. A sense of individuality and being needed were important to some. Few we've surveyed want to be boss, but most seek creative opportunities and work that is personally gratifying.

Of all the things you've done in your life, think about what you've *enjoyed the most* and *enjoyed the least.* After you list them, explain why each gave you either pleasure or displeasure. Did you learn anything from even the negative experiences?

Make a list of your strengths and weaknesses. List all your jobs and what skills you learned in each one. List your most significant achievements and why you think they were important. Remember, it's your opinion that counts in this test. List the most frustrating and/or dissatisfying situations of your life and why. Based on how you've reacted to the preceding lists, analyze your current work situation.

QUALITY CONTROL CIRCLE

Invariably, whenever we mention Japanese productivity or Japanese management methods, our listeners inform us that it'll never work here, explain that we don't understand the great cultural differences between our countries, or give us other variations of "East is East and West is West." We know, we know, but in what follows, we are using Japanese techniques as a jumping-off place from which to launch your ideas of how we might increase our country's productivity. Today's magic word is productivity. The Japanese have it and we don't. But we do have unemployment, job insecurity, price competition, and consumer unhappiness—all of which can be said to be related to product quality to some extent. And product quality is what Japan set out to improve with a vengeance.

One of the methods adopted was the Quality Circle—essentially a training program for directors, managers, supervisors, and technical specialists. At last, it reached the worker, where it was decided that the training would be offered on a voluntary basis. Since 1962, about 3,000 circles or 7 million workers have taken the training in how to improve the quality of the products they produce.

Quality Circles were formed with ten or so workers from different departments seated around a table. They learned quality control by the book and through the use of project exercises designed to teach problem solving, collecting and analyzing data, analyzing competing theories on the causes of product defects, writing reports of findings to management, and similar skills. The motivation remained high after projects were completed and the Quality Circles became self-sustaining.

Do these circles have any application in our country, with its different history, our essentially adversary relationship between labor and management, and the entrenched vested interests of almost everybody? Management has some jealously guarded prerogatives; workers face the possibility of job loss if more efficient methods are found; and workers need some insurance that they will share in any economic benefits that result from improved quality and productivity.

But most people we know are interested in job enrichment. Most people we know also have an idea about how their job should function. As social researcher Daniel Yankelovitch stated recently on public television, "Those who work at a job eight hours a day know what the job requires." In the simplest language, we are talking about worker participation. We believe that no greater motivator exists, all else being equal, than the feeling and the fact of contributing—ideas as well as labor.

For secretaries, try once-a-week meetings and see if together you can't come up with ways of working more efficiently. Write down concrete ways of solving problems and submit the ideas to your boss. Look at the process of how work is produced and see, through work simplification methods, if unnecessary steps can't be eliminated. Discover ways, through problem-solving techniques, to increase job interest, productivity, or worker morale. Resistance may be encountered on any decision making that your boss considers his exclusive province, but perhaps he can be convinced that new ideas on work assignments and problem analysis and recommendations for action won't bring the company (or him) down.

This has been an all-too-brief look at a very complicated subject. If you're interested in the subject, try some research on your own, especially as it applies to office workers. You might also study the Parker Pen Company of Janesville, Wisconsin, which has adopted the Scanlon Plan of worker participation; it's a union shop as well.

8
Getting It Done

LEADERSHIP

Let's assume that you're good at your job. You've got all the technical skills down cold. You exhibit tact, diplomacy, and the right degree of assertiveness. Still, something seems to be missing in this portrait of perfection. Could it be enthusiasm? Enthusiasm seems to us to be the quality that marks a successful leader. It sparks an answering response in others.

A successful leader brings out the best in other people, is decisive, is alert, makes the most of her own abilities, takes an interest in peers and subordinates, communicates clearly, finishes any assigned tasks—and looks for more responsibility. A successful leader always praises in public and scolds in private. Did we mention a portrait of perfection earlier? We didn't really intend to paint one; just to allude to qualities that leaders share, realizing that the essential ones are often mysterious. Enthusiasm, no matter how it's defined, still seems to us the one major ingredient. And you know it when you see it.

If you have that rare leadership ability, one of the things you probably find it easy to do is delegate work. But delegation is a problem to many. They not only don't know how to do it; they don't even know if they should, or even if they want to. Often unfamiliar with teamwork through inexperience, many women take on impossible burdens and expect to do everything alone.

Delegate when you can. Make it easier by requesting work, not demanding it. In the assertiveness discussion we talked about the importance of those small, powerful pronouns, "you" and "we": "We have a problem." "We need to talk about this." And, of course, the magic "What do you think?" Try also not to fob off too many jobs you have little enthusiasm for; it'll be difficult to generate enthusiasm in others. You're delegating, after all—not fobbing off.

One of the ways you might get your boss to delegate to you is by demonstrating your own leadership qualities. You can indeed take on some of his responsibilities through successful application of the management-by-objectives technique.

MANAGEMENT BY OBJECTIVES

It's really not very mysterious: management by objectives (MBO) or management by results (MBR). State agencies practice it; small and large business practice it; schools have adopted it; and maybe even you use it without knowing it. Have you ever planned and executed a dinner party, a family reunion, a birthday bash, or a vacation trip? Put the whole thing into a structure and the whole structure into business language, and by George, you're practicing MBO.

That's an oversimplification, to be sure, but probably only in degree. Learn how to set up goals and objectives for specific tasks and you'll have an opportunity to acquire increased job responsibility. A planning technique, MBO concentrates on results; a motivating force for employees, MBO fits a person's performance into the company's objectives, providing concrete methods of measurement.

For example, a large drug company with the objective of making money has on staff a researcher who wants to find cures for all diseases—a utopian ideal, obviously. But the researcher, by chipping away at his short-term goals year by year, gets closer to the unreachable.

The first step in practicing MBO is to get a written job description. Clerical workers at all levels of employment across the country report that the absence of job descriptions puts them at the mercy of the often all-encompassing "miscellaneous" category or, as it was put to one secretary, "You'll do anything I tell you to." Thorny questions of whether one should do personal chores (of symbolic importance to many secretaries) can often be settled by written job descriptions, plus a little graceful assertiveness. Under ideal circumstances, the job description should be a joint effort between you and your boss.

With your job description in hand, write down what you do in the course of a month, and define those activities that involve planning, organizing, or controlling. Mark them with a P, O, or C. Include any correspondence or phoning you took care of on your own and any work with clients in which you made the decisions. These are all management functions.

So far we've been concerned only with your daily activities, but those activities are just steps toward fulfilling your responsibilities. Now put the corresponding activity numbers under the appropriate part-time job or responsibility. For example, the secretary (Ellen L. Fleming) who made out the list that follows had responsibilities in personnel, administration, clerical work, and communications.

PART-TIME JOBS OR RESPONSIBILITIES	ACTIVITIES
1. Personnel—4, 5, 6, 9, 11, 15, 16, 17, 20, 22, 27	1. Typing
	2. Answering correspondence
	3. Reviewing and routing first-class mail
	4. Handling administrative details for profit-sharing plan
	5. Writing newsletter
2. Administrative—2, 3, 7, 8, 13, 18, 19, 21, 24, 25, 26, 27	6. Social events (office parties, etc.)
	7. Handling phone calls
	8. Handling information retrieval
	9. Writing personnel programs
	10. Doing public relations

3. Clerical—1, 12, 14, 18

4. Communications—5, 10, 11, 15, 20, 21

11. Handling such employee relations as writing announcements
12. Filing and maintaining files
13. Buffering for boss
14. Maintaining IBM copier
15. Updating items on employee bulletin boards
16. Handling paperwork for retiring employees
17. Ordering service awards
18. Making reservations for customer entertainment
19. Handling special projects
20. Updating employee handbook
21. Reading business literature
22. Disseminating pension information
23. Relaying information to boss
24. Controlling phone calls to boss
25. Writing reports
26. Running company errands
27. Collecting donations
28. Entering accounts receivable in journal

With all this information you are ready to write an objective for a job responsibility—one responsibility, one objective. Objectives may be stated in such abstract ways to as improve, to ensure, to maintain, or to increase. Remember that objectives fit into the company's long-range objectives and may never be attained.

Sounds quite lofty, doesn't it? Now get more concrete and figure out *how* you're going to improve (and, of course, *what*), ensure, or maintain. You've got the words. Now set them to music. Criteria or indicators measuring how you'll achieve your objectives need to be written down. "Number of," "percentage," and "time frames" make good indicators. Set one goal for each criterion. Added together, your goals should accomplish your objective. There are both long- and short-range objectives. Each responsibility needs an objective of one year or longer; each goal one year or less.

The following is a form you can use in writing your own objectives. We're including some examples of real objectives written by real secretaries both for their own responsibilities and for a responsibility of their bosses they believed they could assume. The period covered by this form is normally three to six months.

Title: Name the established position.

Purpose: State, preferably in one sentence, and in terms of the desired aim, why the job exists.

Responsibility: A brief description of a major area in which the person is responsible for achieving results.

Objective: Indicates a striving for achievement (improve, ensure). Is long term and relatively broad; Is not an activity (or project).

Criteria or Indicators	**Goals**
Measure how well the objectives are being achieved.	Are set one for each indicator.
In total, cover all aspects of the objective.	Should be challenging, yet attainable.
Should be measurable in specific terms.	Should be specific, preferably quantitative (absolute numbers or percentages.)
Specify the information required to assess the achievement of your objective.	Are set after mutual agreement between your superior and yourself.
Should not exceed five for any one objective.	

Results are to be listed opposite the applicable goals.

Title: Executive secretary

Purpose: To assure that the office of the executive vice-president operates efficiently and to meet all goals within a time frame.*

Responsibility: Administration of travel department

Objective: Establish a corporate travel department

Criteria or Indicators   **Goals**

1. Time frame for research   By November 1

    a. Runways
    b. Airport
    c. Costs
    d. Personnel
    e. Travel priorities

2. Set up system   Year End

    a. Filing
    b. Maps
    c. Survey and travel forms

3. Write policy/procedures   End January
   for corporate manual

Title: Secretary (Pamela Duffy, Helene Cosgrove)

Purpose:

Responsibility: Personnel

Objective: To improve morale throughout the office

* Some secretaries did not spell out purpose. The above description is a good working statement of purpose for most secretaries; they have only to change the name of the office.

Criteria or Indicators	**Goals**
1. Increase percentage of office orientation for new employees	100%

a. Detailed descriptions of office functions
   b. Detailed descriptions of office procedures
   c. Proper introductions throughout the office	

2. Increase knowledge of personnel information on bonds, allotments, and so on, including whom to see	100%
3. Increase knowledge of promotions	100%

a. Criteria more stabilized
   b. More equitable department wide process
   c. Proper training in such skills as job description writing	

4. Increase percentage of secretarial responsibility within the office/division	95%
a. Secretarial meeting (at least once a month b. Secretarial training (at least three courses a year	
5. Increase office recreation (to establish teamwork) with softball teams, games, and similar activities	55%

6. Central office location, with   By 1981
   all offices in the same building

Title: Secretary (Linda Mason)

Purpose:

Responsibility: Correspondence

Objective: To improve flow of response to correspondence

Criteria or Indicators	Goals
1. Read all correspondence	20 minutes each day
2. Read all magazines	1 hour each day
3. Xerox articles for magazines	15 minutes
4. Respond to letters on own	3 each week
5. Gather information for boss's correspondence	30 minutes each week
6. Type up draft of information for his response	30 minutes each week

---

Title: Executive secretary (Caroline Parker)

Purpose: To coordinate executive workload so as to ensure efficient and effective time usage and increased productivity

Responsibility: Public relations

Objective: To assume total liaison between vice-president and international profit center management in divisional public relations

Criteria or Indicators	Goals
1. Correspondence handled without supervision	Replies drafted and dictated to 75% of incoming correspondence

2. Overseas long-distance telephone calls screened/ referred	90% of incoming calls screened and referred
3. Telexes and cables expedited	90% of telexes/cables handled within days
4. Monthly management reports logged from profit centers	1 report from each profit center

---

Title: Secretary, personnel development (Doris Barnes)

Purpose: Provide secretarial support for the identified needs of the personnel development group

Responsibility: Resource consultant

Objective: To increase the effectiveness, efficiency, and ultimately the productivity of our organization

Criteria or Indicators	**Goals**
1. Meetings that need to be changed	Reschedule no more than 5 meetings per week
2. Times assistance is needed for file retrieval	Only 5 times per week within 1 month
3. Phone calls I can handle	Increase by 50% within 2 months
4. Amount of time needed to plan meetings with hierarchy and other co-workers	Decrease time needed by 35% within 2 months
5. Amount of time needed to train someone to run my office	Office run efficiently in my absence with next 2 months
6. Number of times people contact me for assistance	Handle 5 problems within next month

Do these exercises for your own job. then write an objective, criteria, and goals for a responsibility of your boss you think you could handle. Maybe you can't see what job of his you could assume. Here are some examples from secretaries just like you.

Title: President

Purpose: To work with the parent company on all corporate policies and manage and develop all personnel toward the ultimate aim of the company's growth and profitability

Responsibility: Managing MBO program

Objective: To have all personnel included in the MBO program, making sure all goals are realistic and are being reached

Criteria or Indicators	Goals
1. MBO participation	100% after 1 year
2. Set up guidance and introduce program to new employees	1 hour introductory class by end of their first month
3. Complete explanatory brochure regarding program and distribute to employees	100% in 6 months
4. Evaluate goals with employees	80% within 3 months

(Parenthetically, we might add that in our experience secretaries are not included in the MBO programs of any company represented at our seminars.)

Title: National support manager

Purpose: To assist in the implementation and support of data communications systems for major account on a national basis

Responsibility: To maintain and clarify contract administration

Objective: To improve general discharge and handling of responsibility in this area

Criteria or Indicators	Goals
1. Decrease in incorrect or incomplete invoices (billable calls) returned to office	By 30%
2. Increase in my overall familiarity with customer service division/customer contract	25% in 3 months
3. Increase in clear answers to questions asked by field people regarding contract	95%
4. Improvement in clear answers to questions asked by field people regarding contract	Within 3 days
5. Speed in putting together informational materials for distribution to field people to help them understand contract with our customers better	6 weeks

---

Title: Director of personnel

Responsibility: Personnel

Objective: To develop and increase management skills of managers, supervisors, and employees with potential for advancement and to improve their knowledge of the company's products and functions.

Criteria or Indicators	Goals
1. Number of participants	15
2. Courses available	45
3. Sign-up sheets completed	90% within 3 months
4. Courses completed	45% within 6 months

5. Course evaluation forms   60% within 9 months
   completed

Title: President, Marketing Group

Purpose: Oversee all operations and management of the MG

Responsibility: Chairperson, International Sales Meeting Committee

Objective: Well-planned and coordinated ISM

Criteria or Indicators	**Goals**
1. Number of members and when their assignments are made	Select committee of 5 and assign responsibilities by second meeting
2. Number of meetings each month	Meet 1 week for 2 months, 2 weeks last month
3. Time frame to hear from what % of representatives	Determine number of representatives attending in 3 days
4. Hotels to contact for reservations	Contact 3 major hotels to determine what accommodations they have and what they offer
5. Caterers to contact for arranging of meals	Contact 3 major caterers by August 1 and get prices and menus and lead time
6. Number of people needed for plant setup and by when	Form subcommittee of 5 to ready the plant area for the reps by setting up chairs and tables, arranging tours, and handling name tags
7. Number of restaurants that provide entertainment—prepared by last meeting	Complete a list of Raleigh's finest 4 restaurants and places of entertainment by August 1

8. Number of doctors on call and number of special health considerations	Arrange for 2 medical doctors to be on call in case of an emergency with any of the guests. Inquire as to whether any are handicapped in any way
9. Ratio of employees to guests desirable	Choose 1 MG employee to take responsibility for 5 reps and to handle their transportation to and from hotels
10. Number of people on correspondence committee and how often they report	Appoint 2 people to handle all correspondence and communication to and from the invited guests, report any specific problem areas, and give status report at each meeting

Let's recapitulate before you try filling out such a form for yourself:

1. *Title* of the job, yours—or your boss's, if it's one of his responsibilities you're handling.
2. *Purpose* of the job, includes all the responsibilities added together. If two people in a company have the same purpose, the company is overstaffed by one.
3. *Responsibility*
4. *Objective*
5. *Criteria* (*or indicators*) and *goals* that would accomplish objective.
6. *Results* as they are achieved.

With measurable results and achievable goals, increased responsibility and recognition should be yours for the asking. Part of that recognition should, of course, include a raise.

Meredith Gordon, who works for the parent corporation of a chain of food discount stores, outlined her "fascinating" adventure into restructuring her future according to management principles. In her first step she ". . . approached my boss . . . and firmly mentioned that we had neither objectives for me, standards of performance, nor goals for the position I held. We even discussed the fact that I was not on the roles of office personnel, nor was I on the roles for management. After a lengthy discussion of who I was," Meredith continued, "what position did I really hold, what future was there for me, what did the company want from me, what did I want from the company . . ." the following was achieved:

1. Job description established.
2. Classification established for the job: executive secretary reporting directly to the executive vice-president, dotted line reporting to the vice-president of sales and merchandising (the only executive secretary position in the corporation).
3. Standards of performance established.
4. Placement on the management team.
5. Placement in the bonus program.
6. Real definition of the person, position, qualifications, and abilities established.
7. The position defined as management in the corporation roles."

By now you've got the idea. You know your own objectives and your boss's (you should, if you don't). What remains is to put them into practice. As we said at the beginning, it's not very mysterious. What *is* often mysterious to women (although less so than before) is the nature of teamwork.

The research firm of Johnson-O'Conner found, after testing more than half a million men and women for executive skills, that women have higher natural abilities than men. But men excel in teamwork, in goal setting, in taking in the whole environment—in seeing the whole picture. Secretaries who use MBO methods can cover all the bases.

First, teamwork. Examples abound from the field of sports. Football heros (team players) come readily to mind when male athletes are mentioned, but female solo stars such as Billie Jean King dominate women's sports. It's often said that women have a difficult time working with people they dislike, whereas for most men it's just a fact of business life. Hennig urges women to "work with everyone you need, whether you can stand them or not." In other words, be a team player. Part of this is keeping in mind that your goal is getting the job done, and it doesn't matter with whom you work to do it. Learning how and when to delegate is also part of teamwork. You don't have to do everything by yourself to be a "good girl."

Second, goal setting. MBO will teach you how to set up a system for reaching your goals, but you, your work, your boss, and your plans for your future will determine *what* goals to set.

Third, taking in the environment or seeing the organization as a whole; reading job-related business journals, *The Wall Street Journal,* and other business publications, not only to keep current, but also to determine whether or not you're in a section of the country that's growing. Projections, for instance, predict that by the year 2000, Houston, Texas, will be the largest city in the United States. Maybe you'd like to be there. Bureau of Census figures show the West and South have the greatest population growth in the last ten years. What about your company's potential for growth in its present location? Has its product or service got a future?

Finally, a quiz to see how you'd survive as a manager.

MANAGEMENT SURVIVAL

Directions: The following is a randomly listed section of 15 different management steps or activities. Rank them in proper sequence. The first to be undertaken should be ranked No. 1; the second, No. 2; and so on, through No. 15. Place the rank number in the space immediately to the left for each step.

- Provide development and training.
- Establish overall organization policies.
- Prepare position descriptions.
- Clarify position boundaries (laws, budgets).
- Determine authority.
- Establish objectives.
- Clarify relationships.
- Take inventory.
- Establish position specifications.
- Set plans.
- Determine standards of performance.

_____   Determine mission.
_____   Review and rework.
_____   Establish "check points."
_____   Recruit people.

The answers are as follows: 14, 5, 8, 13, 7, 3, 9, 1, 10, 4, 12, 2, 15, 6, 11. Nos. 1 through 6 are planning skills; 7 through 11 are organizational skills; and 12 through 15 involve control.

9
Techniques of Problem Solving

By now, you've mastered all the basics of your job, managed time so adroitly you've discovered another hour or two in the day to communicate to everyone about anything—assertively, if necessary—and taken on more and more responsibility, organizing the jobs MBO style, of course. Are all your problems solved? What could be left? Maybe just the technique of problem solving itself. How do some people go about setting up solutions, and can certain techniques be used to solve problems?

In essence all of Part II has been concerned with problem solving and techniques or skills designed to mitigate problems. Communication principles, time management, work simplification, the setting up of MBOs—these are all professional tools that work. Let's think about the mechanics of problem solving itself—ways of approaching problems that at least give you a chance at solutions.

Cybernetics, computers, complicated phone systems, word processors, visual display terminals (VDTs), are all part of the present and will be an even bigger part of the future. How about synectics? Is it a new miracle machine? No. It's a method of solving problems by setting up analogous situations and seeing if the solution (point of view) used in one situation transfers to another (forced fit)—looking for con*nec*tions between two things and *syn*thesizing them.

For example, Eli Whitney, after observing the movement a cat made as it struck out at a chicken and plucked its feathers, transferred this motion to a piece of machinery and invented the cotton gin. Jonathan Miller, in his book and television program *The Body in Question,* states that only in the last 50 years or so has medicine really become effective because that's the time that's passed since William Harvey, an English physician, first thought to compare the heart to a pump. In other words, the analogy of the body to a machine enables doctors to develop substitute parts and medicines that mimic the muscular and chemical actions of the body.

Seeing analogies is at the root of most creative problem solving. Knute Rockne, the football coach, trained his backfield by a method developed when he saw the analogy between a backfield and a chorus line. What's the "problem" both have? How to move in unison. How can that be achieved? Through music. A chorus line trains to music. Reasoning if it worked for dancers it would work for his players, Rockne thereafter trained his backfield to music. His mind went through the following steps:

1. Statement of problem (how to move in unison)
2. Analogy to chorus line
3. Essence: trained to music
4. Problem solved by training to music

Set up some of your own problems:

	YOUR OFFICE	ANALOGY
Problem	Teamwork: boss and secretary	Teamwork: quarterback and player
Solution	Communicate each day Set priorities	Communicates Calls plays
Problem	Too much paperwork	Overweight person
Solution	Eliminate unnecessary items Work simplification	Eat only to satisfy hunger Establish careful diet

Look for analogies that will help you see connections. See if you can't apply them to your job and your life. Actually, it's kind of fun. Notice that writers do it all the time. Any number of tests that you've taken have undoubtedly asked you what something is to something else. Although it's often not apparent at the time, problems present a creative challenge. First, determine if what you think is a problem actually is one. Next, seek alternative ways to look at and solve the problem. Finally, put your theories into practice. No job or life will ever be free of problems, so consider them opportunities. "If life hands you a lemon, made lemonade," a famous directive goes.

Is it a lemon you've been handed—or a peach? Do you have a problem? Study it carefully; withhold conclusions for a while. Can it be classified as a problem in time management? In communications? What kind of problem is it? Classifying is a way of defining. Ask also if it is a new problem or a recurring one. Has somebody else come up with a solution? Would she help you with it? Is it a high-priority problem? Just how serious is it, anyway? Big guns are not for petty annoyances. Determine how and where the problem started. Does it happen at particular times and places? Is there a pattern? Is it isolated or is it part of a process that's causing trouble? Is it the beginning of a trend?

At this stage, gather data on how frequently the problem occurs. Can it be solved with the existing workforce and materials? Would it involve other people and processes? Is it really a "personality problem?" Do you have any alternatives? Are you dealing as much as possible with facts and not opinions? Go back over everything you've compiled. Will your alternative work?

On to your solution. Review any negative effects. What resources will you need? Is a contingency plan desirable? Do you require help? Are you willing or able to make compromises?

Consider all the ways you habitually look at things, your "frame of reference." It is an invaluable and almost automatic response to situations that saves a lot of time. Just as often it leads to things being done the way they've always been done even if someone discovers a better way. Now look at things in a new way. Break out of your frame of reference. What if you had to invent all the things around you yourself? What if you didn't *know* what they were used for? Could you have been a Columbus or an Eli Whitney or any of the world's "what if" people? So ask "what if" or "why." "Because" is not an answer.

In a simplified form we've set up some problems secretaries frequently mention. Try the form on your own problems: You might stir up some tasty lemonade.

Problem:	No recognition from supervisor.
Root:	No job description; boss's lack of knowledge of what your job entails.
Data:	List all activities, responsibilities, objectives, and results (MBO); research personnel records for a job description/grades.
Solution:	Submit to boss; ask to be upgraded and treated as a professional secretary, part of the management team.
Problem:	How to get your boss to realize that you're part of his team. How to open lines of communication.
Root:	Lack of regularly scheduled job evaluations on a frequent, systematic basis.
Data:	Gather specifics on which you need feedback for your communications problem; aid in solving teamwork problem.
Solution:	Present an evaluation to boss. Evaluate yourself as a secretary; seek boss's evaluation of you as a secretary. Then both of you evaluate your team effectiveness.
Problem:	Confusing directions; frequent changing of priorities.
Root:	Poor communications.
Data:	Has this occurred before? Could someone help with an answer? How many people does it involve—do you have multiple bosses? Is one boss "more equal" than the others?
Choices:	Go with it. Get help. Get sick.
Solution:	Set up a brief morning meeting on a daily basis to determine the day's priorities.

Remember to take nothing for granted, challenge all assumptions, and dream a little each day.

Part III

Looking to the Future

10
What If?

Don't dismiss dreaming. It's a way of asking yourself "what if?" In a sense that's what this is all about, seeing yourself in a new, expanded role: administrative or executive secretary—a professional. And professionals use other professionals to get where they want to go. Do you think that's only for executives? Perhaps you could use a mentor.

MENTORS

A mentor could:
  Sponsor a career move
  Provide visibility
  Teach
  Share information
  Provide protection
  Provide opportunities
  Foster growth
  Be a role model
  Expose you to future possibilities
  Encourage
  Provide acceptance and confirmation
  Counsel and offer friendship

At least that's what the proponents of mentors claim.

Dictionaries define a mentor as "a wise and faithful advisor or tutor." The word comes from the Greek poet Homer's "faithful and wise" Mentor, and implies someone older and more experienced, someone who can guide you on the way up because he or she has traveled the same road. The relationship is one of master and apprentice, and is most often found in the worlds of arts and crafts and academia. Is it of any value to you as a secretary, or are we speaking only of those at the executive level whose mentors are analyzed and graphed by PhDs?

Some experts say have a mentor, by all means; as if you could put an ad in the paper: "Wanted—one mentor for guidance and advice. Must know the pathway to success." That may not be as farfetched as it sounds. Institutionalized mentoring programs have been suggested as a way of systematizing the relationship. Others question their value. Rosabeth Kanter, author of *The Men and Women of the Corporation*, believes finding a single mentor has overtones of finding the right man. Focus on the organization's goals and make it responsible for supporting women to the same degree it supports men, Ms. Kanter suggests, claiming that that route offers more of value to women.

If you know an executive secretary or an administrative assistant who was once much like you, see if she'll give you some pointers, tutor you in the ways of the world you have chosen. A mentor might help, but if you don't have the "right stuff," it probably won't make much difference in the long run.

NETWORKS

Networks, according to an article in a new magazine devoted to women, "have gone national." Certainly they've gone public: Books, excerpts from the books printed in metropolitan dailies, and television interviews with the authors have catapulted what would seem to be an informal mutual back-scratching operation among men into a whole formalized series of networks among women. Are they, or some of them at any rate, anything more than clubs? If so, is that wrong, or just not what the word "network" implies?

Where a club is structured, networks should have fluidity, we believe. Although we're not critical of groups that help and support women, the idea behind networks, borrowed from "the old boys network" (which may or may not exist) is their informality, the almost invisible tie that binds those who have done favors for and have obligations to each other. Of course, women can take that loosely connected system and make it their own. On that basis, we tell you of some networks that might benefit secretaries (all information current in March 1980). As with the mentor idea, use your own good judgment.

National Association of Executive
 Secretaries
9401 Lee Highway
Suite 210
Fairfax, VA 20031

Architectural Secretaries
 Association
1735 New York Avenue NW
Washington, D.C. 20006

Professional Secretaries
 International
2440 Pershing Road
Kansas City, MO 64108
Phone: (816) 474-5755

* Women Employed
37 South Wabash
Chicago, IL 60603
Phone: (312) 782-3902

* Nine to Five
140 Clarendon Street
Boston, MA 02116
Phone: (617) 536-6003

* National Association of
 Government Secretaries
5143 Summit Drive
Fairfax, VA 22030

National Federation of Business
 and Professional Women's Clubs
2012 Massachusetts Avenue NW
Washington, D.C. 20036

Women's Network
39 E. Market St. Suite 502
Akron, OH 44308

What Now? (newsletter)
P.O. Box 17584
San Antonio, TX 78217
Phone: (512) 657-3329

* 60 Words Per Minute
1346 Connecticut Avenue NW
Washington, D.C. 20017

* Women Office Workers
680 Lexington Avenue
New York, New York 10022
Phone: (212) 688-4160

* Working Women
1224 Huron Road
Cleveland, OH 44115
Phone: (216) 566-8511

National Association of Legal
 Secretaries
3005 East Skelly Drive, Suite 120
Tulsa, OK 74105

* Some of the 13 organizations affiliated with the National Association of Working Women.

You might want to start a network of your own. Some suggestions:

1. With two or three other women, list 30 women each that you know and group them by their titles or by their professions.
2. State the purpose and the long-range plan, such as:
   a. Pool of knowledge
   b. Way to meet mentors for role playing
   c. Information bank
   d. Support group
   e. Way to share technical skills
3. Set up a schedule of meetings to be held two weeks or a month apart.
4. Determine needs:
   a. What is the format?
   b. What are the financial needs?
   c. How could you be funded?
   d. Should you provide training for special skills?
5. Your network in the future:
   a. Shall we have lectures?
   b. Shall we affiliate?
   c. How visible should we be?
6. Set up an agenda for meetings and election of officers.

Typical of groups in the National Association of Working Women is Women Employed. Based in Chicago, WE has a membership of more than 1,000. Yearly dues are $15.00, or $28.00 for membership in the secretarial network. WE holds monthly meetings. Activist groups such as these are nonprofit and provide a research center, publications at 20 percent off, a "career connection" if a member is interested in job advancement, and seminars for their members on such topics as assertiveness and office politics. One of their goals is to unionize. Just recently, WE organized a secretarial job bank: Organizations with job openings can fill them from the membership of WE. Job counseling is also offered for such problems as sexual harassment.

SEXUAL HARASSMENT

It is still a problem. Surveys indicate that 70 percent of the women responding to the polls have been sexually harassed at work. Even higher figures have been reported by other surveys. In our seminars, however, we have found that sexual harassment is on the downswing. According to some experts, including Dr. Natasha Josefowitz, an associate professor of business administration at San Diego State College in California, power is behind it all—even behind purely verbal "kidding" of a sexual nature. It's a way some men have, Dr. Josefowitz claims, of asserting and keeping their "dominance" over women. Women who are reluctant or afraid to put a stop to it are "buying" the whole thing, consciously or unconsciously. And if you "buy" it by your silence, you perpetuate the myth that women really like or at least don't mind what is going on.

Some suggestions: Be straightforward, not subtle, and ask the man what you might say or do to convince him that that sort of behavior is *not* all right with you. Be clear and serious; all but the most thickheaded will get the message. If not, there's nothing wrong with anger. Again, be clear and forceful, leaving no room for misunderstanding. Let him know that *this is unacceptable behavior*.

If he still has trouble believing the message he's getting, keep a record of every incident, in detail. Be specific as to what was said, when, and where. Think about comparing notes with other women, but use your judgment about this. Some women have advised against this because they believe it could make you an object of gossip. But it could also be a source of allies.

Another ally, of course, is your company's personnel department or employee relations office. You'll get a hearing. Be businesslike, and assure them that you'll forget the past, but only if the harassment comes to a stop.

Informal surveys we've conducted at seminars, where the subject always arises, indicate that sexual harassers cut across all racial and ethnic lines. Many secretaries tell us that the "worst" are men who are 40 and over, primarily those in the creative fields. Money men and scientists are infrequent offenders, they tell us. And they tell us more—about those who literally chase them around the desk, about the "love" notes left in typewriters, about the pinchers and the pawers. According to recent statistics, more and more women are filing complaints with the Equal Employment Opportunity Commission.

EQUAL EMPLOYMENT OPPORTUNITIES

If networks are one resource available to you, the law of the land is another major one when you are aware of its provisions and how they affect you in your working life. For example, the Equal Pay Act covers all employers who are required to pay minimum wages. The law states that a woman may not be paid at a lower rate than a man who is doing substantially the same work if the jobs require equal skill, effort, and responsibility. The jobs *do not* have to be identical or have the same title. Abuses of this law are now being handled by the Equal Employment Opportunity Commission, Washington, D.C. 20506.

Another significant piece of legislation is Title VII of the Civil Rights Act of 1964. The act, currently the most comprehensive law forbidding discrimination on the basis of sex in the terms and conditions of employment, applies to all private and public educational institutions, state and local governments, and private employers of more than 15 employees. Charges may also be filed with the EEOC.

Then there's the controversial Affirmative Action Program mandated by Executive Order 11246, which prohibits employment discrimination on the basis of race, color, religion, sex, or national origin. Acting on the idea that discrimination in employment can be eliminated when employers take positive steps to identify and change policies, patterns, and practices that cause or perpetuate inequality, affirmative action is designed to end the conditions that produce inequality and discrimination. That's the intent.

The order affects employers having contracts with the U.S. government in amounts of $10,000. Most large corporations have such federal contracts, so they are subject to the order. The EEOC is also assigned to monitor the affirmative action plans required of all federal contractors and subcontractors with contracts over $50,000 and more than 50 employees. Enforcement is handled by the Office of Federal Control Compliance (OFCC), which has overall respon-sibility for approving affirmative action plans and for enforcing Executive Order 11246. Above this agency are the Employment Standards Administration, the regional office of the Department of Labor, and, ultimately, the federal office of the Department of Labor.

Federal guidelines for writing an affirmative action plan recommend having *written job descriptions,* instituting *job posting* so that qualified women and minorities can be promoted, and developing *training programs.*

You could try taking this little test yourself or slipping it to your boss. It's put out by the Equal Employment Opportunity Commission:

An employer:

	TRUE	FALSE
1. Can refuse to hire women who have small children at home.	______	______
2. Can generally obtain and use an applicant's arrest record as the basis for nonemployment.	______	______
3. Can prohibit employees from conversing in their native language on the job.	______	______
4. Whose employees are mostly white or male can rely solely upon word of mouth to recruit new employees.	______	______
5. Can refuse to hire women to work at night, because it wishes to protect them.	______	______
6. May require all pregnant women to take a leave of absence at a specified time before delivery date.	______	______
7. May establish different benefits—pension, retirement, insurance, and health plans—for male employees than for female employees.	______	______

8. May hire only males for a job if state law forbids employment of women in that capacity. _______ _______

9. Need not attempt to adjust work schedules to permit an employee time off for a religious observance. _______ _______

10. Only disobeys the Equal Employment Opportunity laws when it is acting intentionally or with ill motive. _______ _______

The answers to 1 through 10 above are false.

CAREER CHANGE: THE MBA QUESTION

In spite of all we've said, you've decided that being Super Sally, the Successful Secretary, was fine for a while, but you long for greener pastures. What can you do? Many women are going for the master of business administration (MBA) degree. Does it guarantee your future, color those pastures dollar green? If you're after a career in corporate management, according to some people, an MBA is essential. Others say it might be, but you can't generalize.

There is a general consensus that getting that degree takes a lot of time and money. When you've got it, you might edge out a competitor who doesn't have one. Then again, it might depend on whether or not your degree is from the "right" school, such as Harvard, Stanford, the universities of Chicago or Virginia, Columbia, Wharton (University of Pennsylvania), or Sloan (Massachusetts). On the other hand, the "right" school degree may carry more weight with some older established companies. Others frequently look elsewhere for their people, often to the graduates of their own state's business schools. If you're going for your MBA, it pays to look around for your school and check with the American Assembly of Collegiate Schools of Business, which has an accreditation system, before applying anywhere.

Although an MBA is often of undeniable value, so is comparable work experience. That can give you irreplaceable and sometimes more relevant experience. But beyond that, it's vital to consider what you want and what you are, not what you think you should want or should be on the basis of the latest trend. Think about what motivates you, what you really enjoy doing. Maybe you're already doing it.

THE RÉSUMÉ

Just in case, it won't hurt to have your résumé in order. Catalyst, a woman's organization whose national headquarters are at 14 East 60th St., New York, NY 10022, has a *Résumé Preparation Manual* that is a good place to start learning about current practices.

Most résumés follow one of four patterns. There are:

1. The Harvard Business School résumé, the old standby, clear and straightforward.
2. The chronological résumé, which is self-explanatory.
3. The functional résumé, which doesn't emphasize chronology, but highlights your skills.
4. The combination résumé, which, while combining both the functional and chronological, can place the emphasis either way while stressing your more relevant work experiences.

If you're thinking about changing careers, the combination résumé is our first choice, although you must guard against writing your life history if you use it. Look over the samples of all the types we've mentioned in Figures 19 to 22 and decide which best fits your work experience.

You may have noticed several things in studying the sample résumés. They are written in a kind of shorthand that might be termed the Western Union method. They do not use the I pronoun. They contain lots of action verbs. They are confined to one page in length (please follow this rule even if you must have your lengthy résumé copied and reduced). They do not mention salary (but make certain the subject is settled at the job interview). They omit your height, weight, state of health, and marital status—although there's some disagreement on this. You shouldn't list references on the résumé itself, but keep a current list ready to send to any prospective employer on request.

Finally, as Jean Summers says in her book *What Every Woman*

Figure 19.   Harvard Business School résumé.

RÉSUMÉ OF SHANNA WILSON

Medical Center	Home Address:
Suburban, IL 60461	Suburban, IL 60466
Phone: 555-4026	Phone: 555-3003

Job Objective: To work in health services in the area of office management and department administration.

Education:
1976–Present   Governors State University   Park Forest South, Illinois
Attending night classes, working toward bachelor's degree in health services administration.

1963–1964   Northern Illinois University   Dekalb, Illinois
1961–1962   In addition to basic liberal arts courses, studied art, sociology, and psychology.

Business
Experience:
1978–Present   Medical Center
Secretary to Directors of Inpatient and Outpatient Psychiatric Services. Set up and organized office; assisted with formulation of department policies and procedures; liaison with other departments; handled purchasing, scheduling, and orientation of extern rotations to unit; strong patient contact; assisted with coordination of various department activities and schedules; supervised outpatient clerical staff; created forms for department use; responsible for development of statistical records and for billing; familiarity with insurance forms.

1975–1978   Chatham, Inc.   Park Forest South, Illinois
Director of Customer Services. Responsible for Order Department, receiving and implementing orders; responsible for accounts payable/receivable; coordinated purchasing of office and laboratory supplies.

1962–1975   Various work experiences with the following companies:

Allstate Insurance Company	Matteson, Illinois
Council for Community Services	Chicago, Illinois
GAC Properties, Inc.	Miami, Florida
Elaine Revell, Inc.	Chicago, Illinois
Great Books Foundation	Chicago, Illinois
House of Vision	Chicago, Illinois
Dr. B.C. Daniel	Harvey, Illinois
Washington Publications	New York, New York

Personal
Background: Wide variety of interests, including piano, art, pottery, bowling, billiards, ping-pong, roller skating, biking, camping, science fiction, documentaries, dancing.

References: Available on request.

Figure 20.   Functional résumé.

Shanna Wilson
Suburban, Il, 60466
555-4026 (office)
555-3003 (home)

Qualifications and Experience:

Office Skills

Experienced with various office machines, including operation of dry and wet copiers, typewriter (55 wpm), calculator, ten-key adding machine, teletype, switchboard, dictaphone, NCR biller computer, strip-printer headliner.

Writing

Composed much of own correspondence along with supervisor's. Experienced in editing and copywriting for internal sales promotions.

Supervision

Experienced in training new personnel in office procedures and operation of equipment. Managed staff of three editorial assistants.

Public Relations

Much public contact in service areas, both in person and over telephone. Liaison with outside agencies in community. Able to deal with all levels of personnel in organization structure.

Organization

Have had several job opportunities requiring setting up of office, systems, and records.

Administration and Management

Participated in committees for formulation of department policies and procedures. Determined department tasks and responsibilities and their priorities. Developed and maintained department statistical records.

Education:

Northern Illinois Unversity. Two years basic liberal arts, with emphasis on sociology.

Governors State University. Currently working toward bachelor's degree in health services administration.

Figure 21.   Chronological résumé.

Shanna Wilson
Suburban, Il. 60466
555-4026 (office)
555-3003 (home)

Secretary

Work Experience:

1978–Present

Secretary to Directors of Inpatient and Outpatient Psychiatry
Medical Center
Suburban, Illinois 60461

• Set up and organized office
• Assisted with formulation of policies and procedures
• Liaison with other medical center departments
• Supervised outpatient clerical staff
• Coordinated various department activities
• Responsible for scheduling and orientation of extern rotations to unit
• Developed and maintained statistical records

1975–1978

Director of Customer Services
Chatham, Inc.
Park Forest South, Illinois

• Responsible for receiving and implementing orders
• Responsible for accounts payable/receivable
• Coordinated purchasing of office and laboratory supplies

1962–1975

Allstate Insurance Company	Transcription Typist
Council for Community Services	Secretary
GAC Properties, Inc.	Senior Editorial Assistant
Great Books Foundation	Head of Order Department
House of Vision	Receptionist
Dr. B.C. Daniel	Doctor's Assistant
Washington Publications	Typist/Receptionist

Education:

Governors State University, Park Forest South, Illinois
Working toward bachelor's degree in health services administration

Northern Illinois University, DeKalb, Illinois
1963–1964 Sociology Major
1961–1962 Art Major

Figure 22.   Combination résumé.

Shanna Wilson
Suburban, Il. 60466
555-4026 (office)
555-3003 (home)

Administration and Management:	Participating member of committees for formulation of department policies and procedures. Coordinated various department activities and tasks, setting priorities for objectives. Responsible for organizing offices for optimal operation. Functioned as liaison between department, other departments, and outside community agencies. Assisted with hiring and training of new personnel. Supervised clerical staff.
Office Skills:	Experienced with various office machines, including the operation of wet and dry copiers, typewriter (55 wpm), calculator, ten-key adding machine, teletype, NCR biller computer, switchboard console, dictaphone.
1978–Present:	Medical Center Secretary to Directors of Inpatient and Outpatient Psychiatric Services, with administrative assistance provided to Psychiatric Head Nurse and Medical Center Assistant Administrator.
1975–1978:	Chatham, Inc. Director of Customer Services, responsible for receiving and implementing all orders, handling accounts receivable/payable, and purchasing equipment.
Education:	Governors State University, toward bachelor's degree in health services administration.

Needs to Know to Find a Job in Today's Tough Market (another good reference), never send out a "naked" résumé—one without a cover letter aimed at a specific job, addressed to a specific person (personnel offices can help you there). The letter should be on the order of Shanna Wilson's letter (Figure 23). Don't forget to follow up with a letter after any interview you might get. Not only is it good manners, but it also keeps your name alive.

If you are intent on changing careers and find a way of doing so within your organization—possibly through an affirmative action program—be cautious about a "freedom now" leap into too high a position. It could mean failure through inexperience. Take a lower position in your new department instead ("rightful place"), red circle* your salary, and get the necessary training. When you move up, you'll be ready and more successful.

NEGOTIATIONS

Step 1:   Have an objective in mind.
Step 2:   Make an agenda.
Step 3:   Have clearly in mind what maximums and minimums you would accept.
Step 4:   Present facts.
Step 5:   Depersonalize; that is, use such devices as charts, graphs, and reports. When negotiating, it's always best to get away from "personality."
Step 6:   Use trump card last. Don't blurt out your best negotiating point at the very beginning.
Step 7:   Get on neutral ground if possible.
Step 8:   Be ready and willing to make trade-offs.

Whether you're negotiating for a higher salary or pension or for more responsibility, before you start, make sure that your boss is in a positive frame of mind. Simply test the water first. Say "It's a nice day, don't you think?" If he says "It's a lousy day," it's not a good time. Also, start your negotiations after you've done something laudable; for instance, after you've made all the arrangements for

* Your salary will remain what it was before the move.

Figure 23.   Cover letter.

May 12, 1980

Ms. Terry Harrison
Director of Personnel
Mercy Hospital
Address
Suburban, IL 60429

Dear Ms. Harrison:

I recently read in one of our local papers that Mercy Hospital is developing plans for opening a Psychiatric Unit in the near future.

Inpatient and outpatient psychiatry has been my area of emphasis in health services. Now, having the experience of assisting with the development of programs, policies, and office organization from the ground up, I look forward to being able to use my skills in assisting your psychiatric program reach fruition.

I realize that Mercy Hospital has recently experienced much growth toward innovative programs relating to both patient care and employee relations. I would welcome being a part of such growth and having the opportunity to learn additional health services management skills.

My current résumé is enclosed for your informtion. However, I look forward to hearing from you in person so we may discuss areas of specific interest.

Sincerely,

Shanna Wilson

and pulled off a successful meeting or written a report that pleased your boss very much.

Step 1:   Begin with your *objective* in mind. You want an increase in salary.

Step 2:   Next make an *agenda.* You will talk about salary, pensions, and benefits and your place on the organization chart.

Step 3:   You are making $13,000. You ask for $16,000 *maximum* (you have to be realistic). You will take $15,000 (minimum).

Step 4:   Using your MBO, you show your accomplishments.

Step 5:   Using charts, you illustrate the secretarial shortage and comparable salaries of other workers.

Step 6:   Point out the threat of unions.

Step 7:   If possible, avoid talking in his office. Take him out to lunch or use conference room.

Step 8:   You will trade off a higher pension for a higher salary.

While we're still on the subject of job changes, don't overlook the Bureau of Labor *Occupational Outlook Handbook;* Superintendent of Documents, Government Printing Office, Washington, D.C. 20002. For $8.00 you'll get information on rising and shrinking occupations, salaries, the nature of specific jobs, training requirements, and working conditions. Or try your local library, where you can find periodicals such as *Forbes, Business Week, Harvard Business Review,* the *Wall Street Journal,* and the *New York Times,* plus professional publications aimed at the secretary, including, of course, *Secretary,* sponsored by the Professional Secretaries International Association, *Today's Secretary, Women's Work,* and more. Get the library habit. If you can't find it yourself, the research department or the librarian will be eager to help you track down information.

You might want to find a secretarial school—or find out if you want to find a secretarial school. People disagree about the proper education of today's secretary. In high schools, many of those who make up curricula have a hunch that women, especially minority women, learning Gregg shorthand and banging away on manual typewriters will be ill equipped to function in the office of the future.

Beyond high school, is a school like the Katharine Gibbs School, to take perhaps the best-known example, the answer? According to its brochure, Gibbs offers five different programs. One is a one-year course aimed at high school graduates or those with a few college credits. It offers Shorthand I and II, Business Communications I and II, Accounting Essentials, Secretarial Procedures and Administration, Filing, Business and Personal Finance, Contemporary Business Issues, and Personal Development. No previous experience is required. There are also a two-year liberal arts/secretarial program and an eight and a half-month business training course for students with at least two years of college. The fourth is an advanced section of the one-year program for students with some shorthand and typing experience.

An adult training program is given prominent mention by Gibbs. Aimed at developing "entry-level office skills," the course awards participants 15 CEUs (Continuing Education Units). Proof of high school graduation is required for admission.

11

The Future

It's 1985. Having survived 1984 we're now on friendly terms with computers, automation, and electronics. It's the future and it got here faster than it used to. In the office, all the technological marvels of the time are on stage doing their stuff: The star of the show, and a veteran performer, is the word processor. In 1979, the early days of the wonder machine's market expansion, an estimated 250,000 of them were being fed words all over the land. The supporting cast of high-speed printers, micrographic equipment, facsimile machines, optical scanners, and computer terminals, all heralding the death of paper, were in the wings in 1979. In our 1985 office they're giving their all.

It looks much like any office, this 1985 place: carpets (it's that sort of office), furnishings, plants, windows (an important place, remember?), and, of course, people (we haven't replaced them yet). But, according to computer expert J. H. Aitchison, in a speech before the 1979 Systran International Conference, there are no filing cabinets, no typewriter noise, much less paper, little storage space, fewer desks, more tables, but no secretaries. (Wait, don't leave.)

Somebody, either a professional or a manager, walks into the office and begins work; not by using the phone (and the phone is not ringing, either) but by sitting before and using a computer terminal with a keyboard, display tube, and telephone set. A small printer, located outside this office, also serves several other people.

After working for about ten minutes this person calls an administrative specialist, whose services are shared with other professional/managers.

Now, aren't you glad you waited? The administrative specialist appears to have secretarial skills. She or he takes notes in some type of shorthand and later can be seen working at her own terminal as though typing. After giving her a few instructions, the manager turns back to his own terminal. He's determining if there's any mail for him that has been transmitted by others in the same work area, outside the building, or even outside the community. After reading the mail, rapidly scrolling through unimportant items, he answers some by typing in messages.

Retrieving information from electronic files, he scans through them on the screen to see what reports or correspondence have been put together on specific subjects. He's instructing the administrative specialist, by scrolling through the calendars (including his own), to set up meetings of people located in remote places who also use these terminals, and to try for a convenient meeting time either by conference phone or in person.

Finally, reports and letters, printed on the convenience printer, are brought to him. Putting them in his briefcase, he heads for the airport to attend a meeting in another city. Such out-of-town meetings are infrequent now, because most of his business can be transacted via the telephone and display terminal. With the electronic mail and electronic filing system, very little paper needs to be produced. In fact, it's only necessary when there's no access to a terminal and reports and correspondence must be read or referred to.

Aitchison claims that computer and communications technological breakthroughs will so change the way the white-collar worker does his job that they will bring significant improvements in cost effectiveness for all types of organizations. Referring to all office workers, including professionals and managers, as "knowledge workers," he figures them to be about half the workforce. Office productivity has had a 4 percent increase in the last ten years. (Statistics are from 1979–80.) Estimates for office costs, however, are a burgeoning 40 or 50 percent higher for many organizations. Add to this the *decreasing* cost of computers, and their inevitability in the workplace paints either a rosy or bleak picture, depending on your point of view: sterile and vaguely sci-fi 1984ish, or the means for freeing human beings (at least some human beings) from deadening tasks. It's either neatly utopian or a coldly computerized canvas.

And we haven't even mentioned satellite systems hovering above. Will we have communications! Nothing lost; every word, thought, deed, and action will be recorded somewhere by the Recording Angel of the future. Right now, in early 1980, today's less efficient Recording Angel handles about 70 billion pages of information yearly, distributing it mostly among government and business places. Only one page in 100 is moved electronically.

Information is now doubling every ten years. And that's just written information. Some studies claim that "knowledge workers" spend nearly 75 percent of their time in oral communication. Well-structured information could save time and needn't rely on the human memory for retrieval. Computer filing systems that "cut through the superfluous and irrelevant to the right data," in Aitchison's words, would increase the amount of usable information at the disposal of the "knowledge worker."

How will you fit into what has been labeled the "communications society"? Quite well, thank you, with some ifs and some changes in future secretarial education. Secretaries remain in high demand; in 1980 there were 440,000 job openings. Some experts believe that technology will create expanded opportunities, making the job market more open-ended than it is now. Looking to a more differentiated classification, some see a market for word processing secretaries, as we mentioned earlier—highly skilled technically, accurate and grammatically correct, already on the organization chart—and, on another level, the administrative specialist Aitchison spoke of—a paraprofessional, part of the corporate structure. If that will be the case, and it seems likely to us, school yourselves now in office automation systems, procedures, and controls and learn some basic supervisory skills.

Many people, taking a fearful peek into the future, see millions of jobs disappearing or at the least many of today's secretaries performing repetitive mechanical tasks, much like a human processor. We'll place our bets on the skilled secretary adapting to the new opportunities presented and ready to assume the increased responsibilities she's been seeking.

Many executives believe that more of their responsibilities could be delegated if the people to handle the tasks—administrative in nature—were available. And secretaries know they could do the work if their time, sometimes as much as 45 percent of it, weren't consumed by the typewriter, the copy machine (one study discovered that, on the average, six copies are made for every original document, many of them for internal use and storage), the mail, and the telephone.

New systems of office automation, according to many in the field, can free the manager of much administrative detail and the secretary of much routine work. Guess who is waiting to take over some of the boss's responsibilities. You, if you're ready. History has shown that when the machine comes in the door, the manager (usually male) often balks and turns the job over to a female.* It was true of the typewriter yesterday. Today, many managers dislike the intricacies of the new phone systems, for example, and no doubt some will not be happy with a keyboard.

This may be especially true of senior executives not educated in the business machine world. But, some industrial psychologists believe, even with acceptance, most executives need automated systems designed with their personal idiosyncrasies in mind, flexible enough to fit the person and not the other way around. Like the Sabbath, systems should be made for man (woman). Secretaries, in the main, are excited by the new technology, seeing it as a way of lightening their workload and giving them a career path in their own field without requiring them to become something else in order to suceed. The office of the future can mean as well that, at last, a secretary and a boss can function efficiently as a team.

We're back now, back to the world most of us probably inhabit, with a few super typewriters, many clunkers, a copy machine endlessly out of commission or eternally in use, a phone system marvelous in theory but devilish in practice, a monumentally indifferent duplicating department. Functioning in the middle of this are

---

* Since we are primarily pro-secretary no matter what the sex, we shouldn't be, but are, amused to learn that a device called Correct 'n' Spell, retailing for about $1,000 has been developed to detect and automatically correct misspellings and typos in the range of 1 million words. It was developed by Compucorp specifically for male secretaries, who are said to be increasing in number—a not unmixed blessing, according to the company's president, Elmer Easton. Men, he claims, are by and large clumsy and dreadful spellers.

you, the secretary—which might mean that you are a receptionist or that you type letters all day from dictaphone tapes. Remember the Englishwoman, Georgia, telling us that "secretary" is a title in England, earned only after a stint as a shorthand (clerk) typist? As a matter of fact, there's some justification for the theory that the secretarial shortage results from the practice of calling anyone who performs any kind of clerical work a secretary.

Professionalizing the career by applying management techniques on the job is one step a secretary can take to focus her position. Exploring the certification method advocated by the Professional Secretaries International Association is another. After successfully completing a two-day, six-part exam, the secretary becomes a certified professional secretary (CPS). The designation doesn't necessarily guarantee her a higher salary but it may get her an average 15 percent more, according to PSIA's figures. There is no "official" recognition of the certification as yet, but the push is on for this or some comparable kind of professional rating to, in PSIA's words, "promote the professional identity of the exceptional secretary" and help management find qualified secretaries.

A CPS applicant is tested in office procedures and administration; economics and management accounting; behavioral science in business; business law and secretarial skills, and decision making. According to the association, the emphasis is on "judgment, understanding, and administrative ability gained through education and work expeience." An outline and bibliography for the exam plus information regarding eligibility for testing are available through the Institute for Certifying Secretaries, a department of the Professional Secretaries International Association, 2440 Pershing Road, G-10, Kansas City, MO 64108.

An executive we know had some misgivings about certified secretaries. "Who would get one?" he asked. "I foresee trouble." Everybody should have such trouble.

12

The Professional Secretary

You know you're not "just" a secretary, but who else does? You know now, or will, with some study, what motivates you; how to organize your time and your boss's; some basics of management by objectives; some communications principles; how to assert yourself; how to write a résumé; and how to simplify work procedures. You know the uses of a network and of a mentor and how to wear a "strong suit," and you've had a peek into the office of the future.

Gaining public recognition of these and other professional skills through certification seems the next logical step. The CPS test presents an acknowledged vehicle. Ads for secretaries in California, Arizona, and Texas specify the CPS as a job requirement. In 1979 there were 13,124 CPS graduates, and the number is growing. To hold her own against the computer, the secretary needs more in her arsenal than typing and shorthand. Concern is increasing that automation (or its abuse) produces dead-end, downgraded clerical jobs that, in turn, produce stress: human processors processing words and data against the clock.

It's not too late to change that disturbing direction, to take charge of the coming automated age before, as Karen Nussbaum of the Cleveland office of Working Women warns, offices become factorylike places where computers are used as supervisors rather than as tools.

Increasingly, secretaries are developing one of the highest rates of stress around, a malady once considered the province of the high-powered male. It's now likely that it's not power that does you in but powerlessness. Clerical workers and saleswomen have twice the coronary disease rates of other women. Among other similarities, the coronary candidate emerging from the statistics has a job that's going nowhere, is unable to express anger (see Chapter 6), has a controlling, Type A boss (see Chapter 4), or, almost as frequently these days, has a controlling visual display terminal (VDT).

Is there an alternative? Specific skills and attitudes giving the secretary some control over her working life are a place to start. But with no answering cooperation from management, unionization is a sure bet. Rethinking the secretarial role is urgent right now. Some method of according professional status to the secretary who's earned it will safeguard the vital human connection between secretary and boss.

That connection is perhaps best seen between those in upper executive echelons and their secretaries. Displaying a loyalty that often transcends the organization that employs them both, executive secretaries and bosses develop a high degree of synergism. Requiring on the secretary's part "the tact of a diplomat, the flexibility of a politician, the dependability of a banker, the intelligence of a college professor, and the stamina of an athlete," as one anonymous source put it, the job is no match for a computer. In fact, it is difficult to find young, ambitious-for-their-own-glory women to fill that role today. The secretarial shortage attests to that.

The secretary is the organizer of myriad details of corporate and office life. "When my secretary's gone, I go up the wall," an executive told us. "When an executive's away on a trip around here, nobody knows he's gone," a 30-year-veteran secretary claimed. "If I take some extra time at lunch, the place goes up for grabs." "The secretary's job is the hardest job to evaluate," that same lost-without-his-secretary boss informed us. "It's what anybody wants to make of it."

Let's make of it a professional career, with all the concomitant responsibilities and rewards that entails. That's how the future shapes up to us. The alternative would be for the secretary to go the way of carbon paper, leaving the VDT, the word processor, the electronic mail, satellite communications, and fully automated office systems to the employee with an adversary rather than cooperative relationship with the boss. Computers are cold comfort.

Secretary Speakout, sponsored annually by the Professional Secretaries International, in its consensus statement in 1981 gave top priority to compensation for secretaries, along with image and questions of productivity. Stating that "appreciation does not replace compensation," the report argues that:

1. Professional secretaries are not paid in accordance with their worth.
2. The gap between beginning and experienced secretaries' pay is too narrow.
3. Secretaries deserve fringe benefits and "perks."
4. Secretarial salaries should not be secret.
5. Lower standards for secretaries, allowed by management, in turn have sustained low salaries.
6. There is a real need for secretaries to know how to negotiate for their own benefit.

As for image, much has already been said in this book, but it can bear frequent reiteration. "Secretaries must believe in themselves before they can command respect," the consensus report states, and we agree wholeheartedly. They should seek inclusion in management processes. Their role should be identified, starting with specific job descriptions and identification on the organization chart. Lower standards should be ended. Young people, especially, need career counseling and planning to ensure the future quality of secretarial professionals.

Secretary and executive must set and measure their goals and objectives jointly. The report emphasizes that judgment is the key to a secretary's productivity and that management's failure to delegate responsibility, coupled with time spent unproductively in personal tasks for executives, has further hampered the secretary's productivity. We can only add our endorsement of the Speakout's report.

If you're interested in pursuing professional certification, look over the CPS outline in the Appendix. No claims are made that the material will be duplicated in the exam; just think of it as a jumping-off place indicating areas of study.

"Beware, a new woman is born," a secretary wrote us after a

seminar. No longer content with being "controlled" by people, she told us of feeling ready to take charge of her own life. No longer satisfied "mumbling into her hand" that she's "just" a secretary but eager to acknowledge openly her professional worth, she expressed in her letter her need for "recognition and an opportunity for personal growth. Money isn't everything," she stated, "but being treated as other professionals are treated . . . accorded exempt status, job descriptions, work performance reviews, is."

But nothing, unfortunately, is ever simple, especially the secretarial role, whether professionalized or not. It's whatever anybody wants to make of it. And what frequently is made of it is a stew of contradictory ingredients. Although she dislikes the connotations of being a secretary, more than one woman is pleased by the proximity to power the job affords. Others chafe under their powerlessness but, like Rebecca, fear taking risks. Protected by the "just a secretary" syndrome, most nevertheless hate being labeled "ten typing finger" or "my girl" or "office wife," or being patronized as a "good girl" while being required to exhibit the utmost loyalty under extreme conditions. And yet many tell us "I like making things run smoothly for my boss; I enjoy organizing and being responsible."

It's a time of many contradictory signals. We read of a younger, more considerate manager and professional treating his secretary with more consideration (big deal). We hear of the concerns of the women's movement that many secretaries live vicariously on their bosses' success and we hear that many secretaries get satisfaction out of helping the boss to be more productive. We know that's true. On the other hand, reports from personnel offices indicate that more and more applicants declare, "I don't do coffee."

But even as ferment takes place, one thing stays constant—money. Office workers, by and large, have some of the lowest salaries in the country. As reported September 7, 1981 in the Chicago *Sun Times,* according to the 1981–1982 *Office Salaries Directory,* published by the Administrative Management Society, the average secretary earns $253 a week and the average salary for clerical positions is $219. Our concern in this book has been with professionalizing the secretary and so we've been emphasizing advancement within the field and some differentiation among the levels of office workers, but we can't ignore the fact that one out of three women workers holds a clerical job.

At this rate, unionization of clerical workers seems a distinct possibility. In fact, early in 1981, the Service Employees International Union, a unit of the AFL-CIO, and Working Women, part of the National Organization of Office Workers, announced a drive aimed at signing up the country's 20 million secretaries and clerical workers. The campaign will be under the flag of District 925—pun intended.

Will secretaries—professional secretaries, that is—unionize? As we reported earlier, informal seminar surveys we've conducted ndicate they won't. But managers shouldn't bank on that. Society undervalues the care-taking skills—except ritualistically once a year—but hates to do without them. Computers cannot take care of executives as well as secretaries.

We've stated that we're pro-secretary. We've seen the willingness to learn; the desire to be given a chance; the need for respect, recognition, and responsibility among secretaries across the country. We've tried to impart skills that transcend the purely technical, that will remain valid whether one sits before a typewriter or before a VDT. To all bosses, we say get the best secretary you can, professionally certified or equivalently trained; pay her what she's worth; and see that the job has a future. To the secretary we say you're a secretary, a professional. There's no "just" about it.

Appendix

The outline that follows was developed as a study aid for the Certified Professional Secretary (CPS) examination developed by the Professional Secretaries International. Designed solely as a study guide to indicate areas in which secretaries should be knowledgeable, P.S.I. makes no guarantees that the study of this material will ensure a passing grade.

As we mentioned in Chapter 12, "Gaining public recognition of . . . professional skills through certification seems the next logical step" toward a professional identity for the secretary. In some states, the CPS is specified as a job requirement. While certification does not as yet enjoy any official recognition, we believe the time is close for some kind of professional rating system for secretaries.

CERTIFIED PROFESSIONAL SECRETARY EXAMINATION OUTLINE

Congratulations! By having this examination outline in your hands you are taking an important step in your professional development, that of continued education. Whether you use the guide for directed self-study for your own enrichment or as a study aid to sit for the CPS examination, your time will be well spent. Whatever your goal, the Institute for Certifying Secretaries wishes you well.

The Institute for Certifying Secretaries, a department of the Professional Secretaries International Association, presents this outline and bibliography as a means of acquainting candidates with the CPS examination and educators who train secretaries within the scope of the examination. It should be understood that the outlines and the texts for the individual parts are not intended to prescribe exactly the content of the examination; they are intended to indicate the areas in which secretaries should possess knowledge, skill, understanding, and judgment. No claim is made that study of this material will ensure the passing of the examination.

PART I—Behavioral Science in Business

The secretary's role requires daily contact with the public as well as other company employees. Consequently, an understanding of psychology, human relations, group dynamics, and leadership is required. Knowing how effective communications can contribute to success in dealing with people is important.

   I. Understanding the individual
      A. Individuality
         1. Uniqueness of personality
         2. Continuity of personality
         3. Personality changes
      B. The self
         1. Origins of the self
         2. Self-perception
         3. The self and emotional adjustment
      C. Emotion
         1. Emotional development
            a. Inheritance
            b. Differentiation of emotions
            c. Factors in emotional adjustment
            d. Changes in emotional expression
            e. Emotional situations as habits and motives
               (1) Pleasure
               (2) Fear
               (3) Anger
               (4) Attitudes
               (5) Frustration
                   (a) Environmental frustration
                   (b) Personal frustration
                   (c) Conflict frustration
              (6) Anxiety and hostility
            f. Defense mechanisms
               (1) Withdrawal
               (2) Reaction formation
               (3) Sublimation and compensation

           (4) Repression
           (5) Rationalization
           (6) Projection
           (7) Displacement
           (8) Fantasy
           (9) Regression
          (10) Identification
     g. Use of defense mechanisms
     h. Reactions to frustration
           (1) Learned adjustments
           (2) Rigidity
           (3) Aggression
           (4) Fear and anxiety

II. Groups and organizations
    A. Group characteristics
    B. Rewards and costs
    C. Conformity to group norms
    D. Factors affecting conformity
       1. Fear of punishment
       2. Alignment with group's belief
       3. Attraction to the group
       4. Perceived consensus of the group
       5. Orientation to the group
       6. Need for acceptance

III. Motivation
    A. Nature of motivation
    B. Physiological drives
    C. General drives
    D. Deprivation
    E. Learned motives
    F. Complex motives

IV. Learning
    A. Descriptions of learning
    B. Characteristics of learning
    C. Cognitive theories
    D. Retention
    E. Determinants of learning
    F. Types of learning

V. Leadership
    A. Personalities of leaders
    B. Formal and informal leaders
    C. Effectiveness of leaders
    D. Characteristics of leadership

VII. Change
    A. Criteria for evaluating change
    B. Introduction to change
    C. Typical value assumptions
    D. Resistance to change

VIII. Interviewing
    A. Functions of the nondirective approach
        1. Provides clues to the problem
        2. Helps interviewer find relief
        3. Helps interviewer to greater insight
    B. Interviewing techniques
        1. Interviewer releases his feelings
        2. A rational look at the facts
        3. Alternate solutions
    C. Things to avoid
        1. Too much warm-up
        2. Premature judgment
        3. Arguing
        4. Excessive psychologizing
        5. Advice giving
        6. Masterminding
        7. Stereotyping
        8. Halo effect
        9. Nervousness/hostility
      10. Misleading phrases

PART II—Business Law

This part of the examination attempts to measure (1) the secretary's knowledge of these principles of business law as they may operate (and not merely as they are defined) in her workaday world, and (2) her knowledge of the content and implications of the operation of government controls on business. Understanding the historical setting in which these controls developed should be emphasized over names and dates.

Section I—Principles of Business Law

    I. Contracts
        A. Elements
            1. Valid subject matter
            2. Mutuality of agreement
            3. Consideration
            4. Capacity of parties
            5. Form required by law

B. Formation
    1. Offer
    2. Acceptance
C. Types
    1. Quasi
    2. Bilateral and unilateral
    3. Express or implied
    4. Formal and simple
D. Breach of contracts—remedies
E. Statute of limitations
F. Statute of frauds

II. Bailments
  A. Creation and termination
  B. Relationship
  C. Types
  D. Obligations
  E. Remedies

III. Agency
  A. Creation
  B. Types of agencies and agents
  C. Rights and obligations of
    1. Agent to principal and third party
    2. Principal to agent and third party
    3. Third to principal and agent

IV. Employment: Rights and obligations of employers
                  and employees

V. Sales
  A. Nature and form
  B. Transfer of title and/or risk of loss
  C. Warranties
  D. Rights and remedies
  E. Product liability

VI. Real and personal property
  A. Real property
    1. Nature of real property
    2. Acquisition of title
    3. Types of deeds
    4. Landlord and tenant relationship
    5. Mortgages, first and second
  B. Personal property
  C. Disposition of real and personal property (wills, sales, gifts, etc.)

VII. Negotiable instruments
    A. Elements
    B. Types
    C. Transfer
    D. Defenses

VIII. Court procedures
    A. Subpoenas and depositions
    B. Court orders
        1. Cease and desist orders
        2. Writ of mandamus, etc.
    C. Bankruptcy

Section II—Regulatory Legislation

I. Business
    A. Laws governing form, creation, and termination of business entities
    B. Regulation of competitive industry
        1. Antitrust legislation
        2. Federal Trade Commission
        3. Federal food, drug, and cosmetic legislation
    C. Consumer and environmental protection legislation
    D. Uniform Commercial Code
    E. Freedom of Information Act

II. Labor
    A. Federal legislation
        1. Rights
        2. Obligations
    B. Unemployment compensation
    C. Worker's compensation
    D. Equal employment opportunity
    E. Occupation Safety and Health Act

III. Government regulatory agencies
    A. Interstate Commerce Commission
    B. Federal Power Commission
    C. Civil Aeronautics Board
    D. Federal Communications Commission
    E. Securities and Exchange Commission
    F. State public utilities commissions

IV. Patents and copyrights

PART III—Economics and Management

This part consists of two major subject areas: economics (40%) and management (60%). In this part emphasis is placed on understanding the basic concepts underlying Canadian, Jamaican, and United States business operation.

I. Economics
   A. Basic concepts of economics
      1. Private property and the profit motive
      2. Supply and demand—effect on prices and production
      3. Markets—effect on prices and production
         a. Competitive markets
         b. Imperfectly competitive markets (monopoly, oligopoly, monopolistic competition)
         c. Composition of output and allocation of resources
         d. Distribution of income (wages, interest, profit)
   B. National income and its determinants
      1. National income measurement concepts
      2. Determination of national income
      3. Fluctuations in national income
      4. Growth of national income
      5. Current measures of economic performance (output, income, commodity prices, security prices, interest rates, yields, wages/hours, sales)
      6. Public sources of economic information
   C. The financial system
      1. Monetary standards and money supply
      2. Credit creation and credit instruments
         a. Negotiable instruments
         b. Letters of credit
      3. Federal Reserve System and its role, Canadian Banking System and its role, or Bank of Jamaica and its role
      4. Commercial banks
      5. Savings and other financial institutions (savings banks, investment banks, insurance companies, credit unions)
      6. Federal loan insurance agencies (Federal Housing Authority, Federal Deposit Insurance Corporation, Small Business Administration, or Jamaican interest, loans, and insurance agencies)
      7. Banking services
      8. National monetary and fiscal policy
   D. Business involvement in current social and economic programs
      1. Conservation of natural resources

      2. Consumerism
      3. Pollution control
      4. Equal employment opportunity
   E. International trade
      1. Common markets and/or Jamaican Common Market (CARIFTA)
      2. Balance of payments
      3. Balance of trade
      4. International finance
      5. Multinational business operations

II. The nature of management
   A. Forms of business organization—financial characteristics, advantages, and disadvantages
      1. Individual proprietorship
      2. Partnership
      3. Corporation (includes conglomerates, holding companies, foundations)
      4. Syndicate or joint venture
      5. Cooperative
   B. Trends in management
      1. Management development
      2. Use of research in management
      3. Professionalization of management
      4. Information theory in management
      5. New concepts (including metric measurements, systems approach)

III. Functions of management
   A. Decision-making processes
      1. Logical reasoning
      2. Quantitative analysis techniques
         a. Use of statistics
         b. Operations research
         c. Decision tables
      3. Graphic techniques
         a. Description
         b. Construction
         c. Interpretation
      4. Brainstorming
   B. Planning
      1. Planning principles
      2. Policy formulation
      3. Management by objectives
   C. Organizing
      1. The organization process
      2. Principles of organization

3. Authority, responsibility, accountability, and cross-functional relationships
4. Tools in organizing—charts and manuals
D. Directing
1. Role of the supervisor
2. Role of the subordinate
E. Controlling
1. The control process
2. Standards and standardization—quantity, quality, cost, and time standards
3. Communication
a. Policies and procedures
b. Meetings
c. Feedback
4. Management by exception

IV. Fields of management
A. Personnel management and labor relations
1. Occupational trends and the nature of the labor force
2. Job analysis, job description, and job specifications
3. Job evaluation
4. Recruiting and selecting
5. Training and development
6. Employee merit evaluation and promotion
7. Wage and salary administration (incentive and nonincentive plans), wage controls
8. Employee benefits (including pension and retirement plans, health and welfare plans, and insurance)
9. Employee suggestion systems
10. Grievances, discipline, absenteeism, tardiness, etc.
11. Collective bargaining
B. Production management
1. Facilities
2. Materials—procurement, processing, and control
3. Methods and quality control
4. Planning and scheduling
C. Marketing management
1. Marketing policy
2. Advertising
3. Sales analysis and control
4. Market analysis of consumer behavior
5. Transportation—traffic management functions (economical and efficient procurement and arrangement of all transportation services)

PART IV—Accounting

(80% Definition/Theory, 20% Computations)

The accounting examination attempts to measure (1) knowledge of the elements of the accounting cycle; (2) ability to analyze financial statement accounts; (3) ability to perform those arithmetical operations associated with accounting, computing interest and discounts; and (4) summarizing and interpreting financial data.

I. Principles and procedures
    A. Theory and classification of accounts
        1. Assets
        2. Liabilities
        3. Owners' and stockholders' equity
        4. Revenue, expense, and income
    B. Accounting cycle
        1. Analyzing transactions and recording
        2. Posting
        3. Trial balance
        4. Work sheet
        5. Financial statements
        6. Adjusting and closing entries
        7. Postclosing trial balance

II. Balance sheet accounts
    A. Accounting for cash income and expenditures
        1. Cash receipts
            a. Cash receipts records
            b. Internal controls
        2. Cash disbursements
            a. Cash disbursements records
            b. Trade and cash discounts
            c. Imprest petty cash
                (1) Establishing petty cash fund
                (2) Replenishing petty cash fund
                (3) Reconciling petty cash
            d. Types of checks and check registers
            e. Voucher system and the recording of accounts payable
            f. Internal controls
        3. Bank statements and cash balance
            a. Reconciliation
            b. Detection and correction of errors
            c. Journal entries to record reconciling items
    B. Accounting for investments
        1. Real estate

2. Bonds and interest income
3. Stocks and dividend income

C. Inventories
  1. Pricing
    a. Last In–First Out (LIFO)
    b. First In–First Out (FIFO)
    c. Weighted average
  2. Applying lower of cost or market theory
  3. Determining cost of goods sold
  4. Evaluating effect of inventory on net income

D. Property, plant, and equipment records
  1. Acquisition costs
  2. Allocation of costs (depreciation, depletion)
  3. Replacements and repairs
  4. Disposition of property items

E. Other assets
  1. Receivables
    a. Notes receivable
      (1) Interest and noninterest bearing
      (2) Discounting
    b. Accounts receivable and bad debts
  2. Prepaid expenses
    a. Insurance
      (1) Types
        (a) Property
        (b) Casualty
        (c) Life and health
        (d) Fidelity and surety insurance bonds
      (2) Co-insurance
      (3) Insurance record maintenance
    b. Supplies
  3. Intangible assets and amortization

F. Debt equities
  1. Short-term obligations
    a. Notes payable
      (1) Types
        (a) Interest bearing (simple and add-on
            interest
        (b) Noninterest bearing
        (c) Term
        (d) Installment
    b. Accounts payable
    c. Accruals
  2. Long-term obligations
    a. Notes

        b. Mortgages
        c. Bonds
    G. Owner's equity
      1. Proprietorship and partnership
      2. Capital stock (rights and responsibilities)
        a. Preferred and common stock
          (1) Characteristics
          (2) Recording the issue of retirement (par, no-par)
          (3) Dividend payments
        b. Treasury stock
        c. Securities markets
          (1) Stock exchanges
          (2) Private placement
      3. Retained earnings
        a. Appropriated
        b. Unappropriated

III. Income statement accounts
    A. Revenues
    B. Expenses
      1. Operating (payroll, payroll taxes, insurance, etc.)
      2. Federal income taxes
        a. Ordinary income/loss
        b. Capital gains/losses

IV. Analysis and interpretation of financial statements
    A. Balance sheet
    B. Operating statements
    C. Retained earnings statement
    D. Statement of changes in financial position (funds flow)
    E. Cash flow statements
    F. Comparative statements
    G. Ratios, percentages, and turnovers

V. Managerial accounting
    A. Cost analysis
      1. Determining unit costs
      2. Variable and fixed costs
      3. Breakeven charts (cost–volume–profit analysis)
        a. Construction
        b. Use and interpretation
    B. Budgets
      1. Types
      2. Factors considered in preparation
      3. Budget variation and analysis

C. Forecasting
  1. Types
  2. Factors considered in preparation
  3. Pro-forma statements

PART V—Secretarial Skills and Decision Making

Secretarial Skills and Decision Making is an in-basket exercise and performance test designed to measure selected skills and decision-making abilities.

Part V contains two sections:

A. Approximately 15 to 20 in-basket items to be grouped according to priorities within half an hour.
B. Approximately 5 to 10 production items to be completed within an hour and a half that will measure the candidate's proficiency in
  1. Note taking from oral instructions
  2. Transcribing timed office-style dictation (80–100 wpm)
  3. Composing at the typewriter
  4. Editing and/or abstracting
  5. Typing tabular or statistical copy

Basic English usage is an integral part of each of the above items.

PART VI—Office Procedures and Administration

This part is to cover in content the subject matter that is unique to the secretary's job. It covers both the traditional and the newer duties created by business data processing, communications media, advances in office management, records management, office systems, and office landscaping.

  I. Secretarial planning
    A. Time sense
    B. Coordination with others
    C. Arrangement of work area
    D. Job manual

  II. Public relations
    A. Receiving visitors
    B. Handling telephone communications
    C. Dealing with the media

  III. Executive travel
    A. Itinerary
      1. Source books and agencies
      2. Tickets, travel, and credit cards

      3. Documents and credentials
      4. Knowledge of travel conditions, facilities, and prefer-
          ences
    B. Reservations
      1. Hotel rooms
      2. Conference facilities
    C. Organization of materials for trip
    D. Communication with executive during trip
      1. Locating executive
      2. Forwarding selected correspondence
      3. Notifying of any significant changes
    E. Preparation of material for executive's return
    F. Follow-up
      1. Expense reports
      2. Special reports and letters of appreciation

IV. Office administration
    A. Organization
      1. Control of clerical services
      2. Techniques of office management
      3. Work environment
        a. Office landscaping
        b. Devices for minimizing fatigue and boredom
    B. Work simplification
      1. Analysis of functions (purchase orders, sales orders,
          invoices, payroll, etc.)
      2. Design of system
        a. Operations chart
        b. Movement diagram
        c. Procedures
          (1) Selecting, requisitioning, and maintaining
              office supplies and equipment
          (2) Perpetual inventory methods for supplies
          (3) Mailroom activities
             (a) Requirements and basis for choice of class
             (b) Special postal services
             (c) Metered mail (equipment and regulations)

 V. Word processing
    A. Systems
    B. Equipment
    C. Positions
    D. Trends

VI. Records management
    A. Analysis of records and records systems

Recommended Reading

Affirmative Action and Equal Employment: A Guide Book for Employers, U.S. Equal Employment Opportunity Commission. Washington, D.C., 1974.

Effective Communication on the Job, William K. Fallon (ed.). New York: AMACOM, 1981.

The Elements of Style, William Strunk, Jr., and E.B. White. New York: MacMillan, 1979.

Golden Guide, Benson & Hedges (Overseas Ltd.). Impact Litho.

How to Get Control of Your Time and Your Life, Alan Lakein. New York: Peter H. Wyden, 1973.

Management, Peter Drucker. New York: Harper & Row, 1974.

The Managerial Woman, Margaret Hennig and Anne Jardin. Garden City, N.Y.: Anchor Press/Doubleday, 1977.

The Motivation of Work, Frederick Herzberg, B. Mausner, and B. Snydeman. New York: John Wiley, 1969.

Pink Collar Workers, Louise Kapp Howe. New York: paperback edition, Avon, 1978; hardcover edition, G. P. Putnam's Sons, 1977.

Step-by-Step Bookkeeping, Robert C. Ragan. New York: Sterling Publishing Co., 1979.

The Time Trap, Alec R. Mackenzie. New York: AMACOM, 1972.

Type A Behavior and Your Heart, Meyer Friedman and Ray Rosenman. New York: Knopf, 1974.

ENDED READING

pretarial Handbook, Anna L. Eckersley-Johnson. Spring-
Mass.: G. & C. Merriam Co., 1976.

*very Woman Needs to Know to Find a Job in Today's Tough Mar-
,* Jean Summers. New York: Fawcett, 1980.

*I Say No, I Feel Guilty: How to Cope—Using the Skills of Systematic
sertive Therapy,* Manuel J. Smith. New York: Dial Press, 1975.